CELEBRATING YOUNG WOMEN

Creative Programs for

New Beginnings

Evening of Excellence

Young Women Values

by
Kathy Thompson

Covenant Communications, Inc.

To my husband, Rick, and my children, Brian and Brandon.

Published by Covenant Communications, Inc.
American Fork, Utah

Copyright © 1997 by Kathy Thompson
All rights reserved

Printed in the United States of America
First Printing: August 1997

04 03 02 01 00 99 98 97   10 9 8 7 6 5 4 3 2 1

ISBN 1-57734-135-x

TABLE OF CONTENTS

GENERAL SUGGESTIONS
For Use with This Book

1. MAKING CHANGES
Suggestions are given in this book for each program, including program outline, decorations, refreshments, etc. Use these ideas, but please remember, you have wonderful ideas, too. Don't be afraid to use your own creative talents to adapt program outlines, skit scripts, or anything else that you feel needs to be changed to better fit the needs of the young women in your ward.

2. INVOLVING THE YOUNG WOMEN
The young women tend to become more excited about a program when they are involved in the planning and preparation of it. Let them share ideas with you. Let them help decorate for the program. They will enjoy helping and it will relieve you of some of the work.

Laurel Project

3. PROVIDING PERSONAL PROGRESS OPPORTUNITIES
The Laurels are always looking for different ideas for their Laurel projects. Here's an idea: Under your direction, let them plan and execute the New Beginnings or Evening of Excellence programs in this book. One Laurel could work on one area of a program while another works on a different area. For example: For the New Beginnings program, "Pattern Your Life After Christ," one Laurel could easily spend twenty hours researching quotes, poems, stories, etc., to put in the suggested notebooks (see p. 4), while another Laurel could organize the skit. This will take some of the work away from you and it will also teach the Laurels how to plan a program.

GENERAL SUGGESTIONS
For Use with This Book

4. MAKING THE INVITATIONS AND HANDOUTS
Most young women enjoy crafts, creating invitations and programs, etc. Plan an activity night a couple of weeks before the program to make the invitations and handouts. Bring all the supplies you need and let the young women make their own. (If the young women want to color the invitations or handouts, run them off on white paper instead of the suggested color.) The harvest garlands from the Evening of Excellence program, "Celebrate a VALUE-able Harvest" (see p. 133) would be fun to let the young women make. After they make each object for their garland, collect and save them. Pass them out at Evening of Excellence or as they earn them.

5. MAKING THE PROGRAMS
When making the programs, make one copy of the program front on white paper. Write or type the words to the opening and closing songs on the blank side of the program front. Use this as the master copy to run off on the suggested colored paper. When the program is folded, the words to the songs will be on the back. This will make it easier for you and your guests during the program because you will not have to run all around the church building trying to find enough songbooks for everyone.

NEW BEGINNINGS

"PATTERN YOUR LIFE AFTER CHRIST"

"...that we may present every man perfect in Christ." *Colossians 1:28*

OBJECTIVE:

To help each young woman and her parents to better understand the Young Women values and to instill a desire in her to work on her personal progress value experiences.

MATERIALS NEEDED:

An invitation for each young woman to be invited, see pp. 13-14

A program for everyone to be invited, see pp. 15-16

A handout for everyone to be invited, see pp. 17-24

A notebook for each young woman to be invited (optional), see p. 4

A copy of the "Jesus Showed Me the Right Pattern" skit for the director and each participant, pp. 6-12

Props and costumes for the skit

PREPARATION:

1. Make the assignments using the suggested Program Outline/Assignment Sheet, p. 5.
2. Assign the parts for the skit.
3. Schedule practice times for the skit, including a dress rehearsal.
4. Assign the speaker.
5. Assign young women to present the values, see p. 4.
6. Talk with your bishopric to ensure their representation at this event.
7. Schedule the church building for the evening of the event, allowing enough time to set up and decorate the afternoon of the event.

SUGGESTIONS FOR DECORATIONS:

1. Have a table set up with a sewing machine and sewing supplies (for example, scissors, a jar of buttons, spools of thread, fabric pieces, etc.)

2. Most fabric stores give away old pattern books and you can purchase used patterns from thrift stores. Set some of these on the table along with the other items.

3. Enlarge the "value" pictures, pp. 26-32, onto 11" x 17" white paper. Use colored pencils to color each picture. Cut out the pattern pieces from old or used patterns. Hang each value picture on the wall in a grouping with five or six of the pattern pieces around it.

SUGGESTIONS FOR REFRESHMENTS:

Sheet cake with punch to drink. (Optional: Copy one of each "value" pattern piece, pp. 18-24, onto the appropriate color of paper. Glue or tape each one to a toothpick or a drinking straw and insert them into the cake to display the values.)

SUGGESTIONS FOR NOTEBOOKS:

1. New Beginnings is a great time to supply each young woman with a notebook that she will keep for all of her years in Young Women. This provides a place for her to write down her goals and to put her personal progress certificates or any other information she wishes to keep. For example, if she obtains a poem about using her talents, she can keep it in her notebook under the heading of "Individual Worth."

2. Purchase a notebook for each young woman. (The notebook needs to have a clear plastic front cover that allows you to insert a sheet of paper.)

3. Purchase seven clear plastic top loading sheet protectors for each notebook, to use as value header pages (see #4 below). You may also want to purchase nine more sheet protectors for each notebook to use for Reports of Progress and Age Group Recognition certificates, or you may add these to each notebook as needed.

4. Copy the "Celestial Patterns" coversheet on p. 25, onto the desired color of paper. (Choose a color that blends well with the notebook.) Copy the "Values," pp. 26-32, onto the appropriate color of paper for each value. Place the "Celestial Patterns" page in the plastic cover on the notebook front. Place each "Value" page in a sheet protector and place the sheet protectors into the notebook in the correct order of the values.

5. (Optional) Research and obtain poems, scriptures, quotes, etc. Copy these and place in each notebook under the appropriate value heading.

6. (Optional) Make a yearly calendar of your Young Women events and activities. Place one in each notebook.

7. (Optional) Make a copy of your Young Women roster including each girl's name, address and phone number. Place one in each notebook.

SUGGESTIONS FOR THE PRESENTATION OF VALUES:

1. Cut out pattern pieces from old or used patterns. Glue two pattern pieces onto poster board. Cut the poster board out around each pattern piece. Use a black marker to write the value title and definition (see Personal Progress book, p. 7) on one pattern piece and the scripture for that value on the other pattern piece. (Or glue a typed printout of the information onto each pattern piece.) Repeat for each value.

2. Have each young woman hold up the corresponding pattern piece as she recites the information for the "Presentation of the Values" during the event. (Hint: Glue a typed printout of the information onto the back of each pattern piece to help each young woman remember her part.)

"PATTERN YOUR LIFE AFTER CHRIST"
Program Outline and Assignment Sheet

or Rainbow of Colors

_____Opening song: "I'm Trying to Be Like Jesus," *Children's Songbook*, p. 78

_____Opening prayer

_____Welcome: Include the objective of the program.

_____Presentation of the Values: To be given by the young women (see p. 4)

_____Presentation of the "Jesus Showed Me the Right Pattern" skit

_____Speaker: Be sure to include these points:
> *We should try to act as Christ did and use his life as an example for our own. (The First Presidency message, "Think on Christ," by President Ezra Taft Benson in the April 1994 issue of the *New Era,* p. 4, may be a good resource for this talk.)
> *By working on and developing our personal progress values, we are becoming more like Christ.

_____Musical number: Allow the young women to choose and sing their favorite song as a group.

_____Closing remarks: Distribute the "Pattern Your Life After Christ" handouts and the notebooks.

_____Closing song: "Come, Follow Me," hymnbook, p. 116

_____Closing prayer and blessing on the refreshments

_____Refreshments: Sheet cake and punch to drink

Also introduce new young women (1) Ashley (2) Krista (3) Mandy (4) Jenny etc.

More Assignments to Consider

_____Preparation of invitations   _____Refreshments organizer
_____Preparation of programs   _____Decorations organizer
_____Preparation of handouts   _____Setup organizer
_____Preparation of notebooks   _____Cleanup organizer
_____Skit director/organizer

INSTRUCTIONS FOR MAKING THE INVITATIONS, PROGRAMS AND HANDOUTS

INVITATIONS: See pp. 13-14.

PROGRAMS: Make a copy of the program border (p. 16). Write or type your program information inside the border. Copy the program front (p. 15) onto ivory paper with the border on the reverse side of the paper. Fold in half. Place a sticker of Christ where indicated.

HANDOUTS: See pp. 17-24.

PLAYERS:

Ashlee - a young woman who will sing a solo
Sarah, Janelle, Mirazz, Amber, Ann, Leann and Andrea - young women who will sing as a group
Mom - a woman's voice from behind the scenes

PROPS YOU WILL NEED:

Sewing machine, scissors, dress pattern and pattern instruction sheet, a finished dress, fabric similar to the finished dress, a set of scriptures, a cellular phone for each girl (only Ashlee's has to really work), a Personal Progress book for each girl

SETTING:

A girls' slumber party at Ashlee's house. The girls could wear pajamas and bathrobes. Set the scene to look like a bedroom with sleeping bags and bean bag chairs. A sewing table should be set up in the room. Throughout the skit the girls should be doing typical slumber party actions—curling each other's hair, polishing their nails, reading magazines, etc. (Hint: Copy the lines for each girl and tape inside a magazine for her so that during the skit she can refer to it to help her remember her lines.)

Ashley **SARAH:**

(teasingly) Guess who asked Mirazz to the prom?

ALL GIRLS EXCEPT MIRAZZ AND SARAH:
Who?

Mandy **JANELLE:**

(with surety) I'll bet it was Jared!

Amber **MIRAZZ:**

(shakes her head to indicate no) No, it was Derek!

Jenny **AMBER:**

(unbelieving) No way! He's so cute!

Angel **ANN:**

(dreamily) I hope Brian will ask me!

Melissa **LEANN:**

(jokingly) I think Brandon has been trying to ask me. Every time I see him in the hallway at school, he looks at me but then turns kind of green!

Trina **ANDREA:**

(teasingly) Ashlee wants Jason to ask her. *(Andrea holds up a dress pattern.)* Look, she's even bought the stuff to make a new dress!

ASHLEE:

(disappointedly) I thought he would, but he hasn't. I guess it's just as well. I can't sew anyway. At least now I don't have to make the stupid dress.

Ashlee's phone begins to ring. All the girls pick up their cellular phones.

ASHLEE:

It's mine.

JANELLE:

(teasingly) See, there's Jason now!

ASHLEE:

(sarcastically) Yeah, right! *(Ashlee answers her phone.)* Hello. *(Becomes very excited but tries not to act too excited)* Hi... um, fine... me too... um, really... I mean, okay. That'd be fun. Bye.

MIRAZZ:

(boldly) So... who was it!

ASHLEE:

(surprised) That was Jason and he asked me to the prom!

All the girls scream with excitement.

AMBER:

It looks like you've got a dress to get started on. *(Ashlee gets a worried look on her face.)* Don't worry, we'll help. Get the instructions out.

Ashlee pulls the instruction sheet and pattern pieces from the pattern envelope, looks at the instructions for a moment, then looks even more worried.

ASHLEE:

Place on the straight grain?... Cut where?... Sew what to what?... Seam allowance? What's that?

Song: "I Look at Instructions and What Do I Find?" sung by Ashlee with the other girls as backup (see p. 11)

ASHLEE:

(very frustrated) Oh, I'll never be able to make this dress!

ANDREA:

(encouragingly) Sure you will. Just have a little faith.

ANN:

(seriously) Andrea's right. You know faith is one of our Young Women values. Christ showed us how to use faith. It was through faith that he was able to heal the sick, make the blind see and accomplish other miracles while he was here on the earth.

Song: "With Faith Applied," sung by all the girls (see p. 12)

ASHLEE:

(She lays the pattern pieces on the fabric and pretends to cut out her dress.) You know, my mom sews all the time. She told me that if I just follow the instructions, my dress will turn out the best I can make it.

LEANN:

(hopeful) Yeah, and with practice, maybe even perfect!

AMBER:

(wondering) Speaking of perfect... In seminary this morning Brother Jones said that Christ said we need to be perfect just as he is. Do you think that's possible?

SARAH:

(seriously) Well, maybe not in this life, but if you think about our Young Women value of divine nature, it seems possible some time. We all have the same divine qualities of Christ; we just need to work to find and develop them. We can be doing that now by following Christ's example.

Song: "We Will Follow," sung by all the girls (see p. 12)

ASHLEE:

(She pretends to sew for a moment, acting as if she is catching on to it and even enjoying it.) Wow, this sewing stuff doesn't seem so hard after all! I must have a talent for it.

JANELLE:

(jokingly) If you want to get even better at it, you can sew my prom dress, too!

MIRAZZ:

(seriously) Janelle's got a good point. Our Young Women value of individual worth reminds us that we each have different talents. Christ told us in a parable that we need to share these talents, not hide them, in order to grow.

Song: "Use Our Talents," sung by all the girls (see p. 12)

ASHLEE:

(excited) Look, you guys! My dress is turning out so great! I can't believe how much fun learning something new can be!

LEANN:
(jokingly) Really! Obviously you've never been to my math class!

AMBER:
(seriously) Gaining knowledge is not only fun but it's also one of our Young Women values. Christ set the example for us. He was only twelve years old when he amazed the scholars at the temple with his knowledge of the gospel. If we pray and work for more knowledge, the Lord will help us to get it.

Song: "Seek For Knowledge," sung by all the girls (see p. 12)

ASHLEE:
(happily) I almost decided to buy a dress. I'm glad now that I chose to sew one instead. I got the color I wanted and saved money too!

MIRAZZ:
(jokingly) Ashlee, you saved money? You did make a good choice. And by the way, could I borrow six dollars for the movies tomorrow? *(Mirazz puts her hand out as if to get the money and Ashlee shrugs her off.)*

ANDREA:
(seriously) We all have to make choices everyday. Our Young Women value of choice and accountability reminds us that we are responsible for those choices. Christ had to make choices. In the desert, Satan tempted him, but Christ made the choice to follow Heavenly Father instead. Just as the instructions told you to put your pattern piece on the straight grain, Christ taught us to put our lives on the straight and narrow path by making wise choices.

Song: "Straight and Narrow," sung by all the girls (see p. 12)

ASHLEE:
(enthusiastically) I just had a great idea! Now that we know how to sew, let's make some children's clothes or baby blankets.

ANN:
That would be fun and we could donate them to a charity.

SARAH:
Great idea! We could do it as a good works goal for our Young Women personal progress.

JANELLE:
(seriously) We should do service for others. Christ showed a great example of service and humility when he washed the feet of his disciples. Christ told us that we should let our light shine in service to others.

Song: "Let Our Light Shine," sung by all the girls (see p. 12)

ASHLEE:
Well, my dress is done. *(Ashlee holds up the finished dress.)* What do you think?

ALL GIRLS MAKE COMMENTS LIKE:
Looks great! Good job! I love it! etc.

ASHLEE:
(teasingly) I hope you guys are being honest with me. Remember, integrity is a Young Women value, too!

LEANN:
(seriously) Integrity does mean being honest in all we say or do. It also means doing the right thing even if it is very hard to do so. Christ showed integrity even at the end of his life. He knew he would suffer tremendous pain in Gethsemane and on the cross, but because of his great love for us and for Heavenly Father, he did what he knew was right.

Song: "Integrity," sung by all the girls (see p. 12)

SARAH:
(excited) Ashlee, your mom was right! We read the instructions and followed the pattern and your dress turned out the way it was supposed to!

ASHLEE:
(seriously) She was right, but you guys have taught me something very important, too—that Christ has given us instructions, the scriptures. *(Ashlee holds up scriptures.)* He has also set an example and given us a pattern of values to live by that will help us to become more like him.

Song: "Jesus Showed Me the Right Pattern," sung by all the girls (see p. 11)

ANN:
(enthusiastically) I'm going to look in my Personal Progress book and start making new goals. *(Ann holds up her Personal Progress book.)*

ANDREA:
Can I work on some goals with you?

ANN:
Sure!

ALL THE GIRLS:
We're going to work on them, too! *(All the girls start to look in their personal progress books and talk as if they are making new goals.)*

MOM:
(a voice from backstage) Girls, it's getting late. Time to turn off the lights and go to sleep now.

ASHLEE:
(disappointedly) Oh, Mom.

The lights go out as the girls keep on talking among themselves. The curtains close.

SONGS

"I Look At Instructions," sung to the tune of "Popcorn Popping," *Children's Songbook,* p. 242

(Ashlee)	I look at instructions and what do I find?
(girls)	What does she find? *(repeat tune of the second measure)*
(Ashlee)	Information that just boggles my mind!
(girls)	Boggles her mind! *(repeat tune of the fourth measure)*
(Ashlee)	I could take scissors and make a cut, up, across, down, oh, I'm such a nut!
(girls)	She could take the scissors and make a cut, up, across, down, no, you're not a nut!
(Ashlee)	There doesn't seem to be,
(girls)	Surely there must be,
(Ashley)	Something written here to help and guide me.

"Jesus Showed Me the Right Pattern," sung to the tune of "Jesus Wants Me for a Sunbeam," *Children's Songbook,* p. 60

(Ashlee)	Jesus showed me the right pattern,
	To live my life each day.
	With ev'ry thread, try to stitch all,
	The values that he gave.
(everyone)	His pattern of values,
	Jesus showed me the right pattern.
	His pattern of values,
	I'll live his pattern each day.

VALUE SONGS: Each value song is sung by all the girls in the skit to the tune of "A Happy Family," *Children's Songbook,* p. 198.

FAITH
"With Faith Applied"
With faith applied, when we ask,
He will help us with the task.
He loves us and showed the way,
To live this value ev'ryday.

DIVINE NATURE
"We Will Follow"
We will follow in his line,
'Cuz our nature is divine.
He loves us and showed the way,
To live this value ev'ryday.

INDIVIDUAL WORTH
"Use Our Talents"
Use our talents, they will grow,
And our great worth we will know.
He loves us and showed the way,
To live this value ev'ryday.

KNOWLEDGE
"Seek For Knowledge"
Seek for knowledge, we will find,
Doors will open in our minds.
He loves us and showed the way,
To live this value ev'ryday.

CHOICE AND ACCOUNTABILITY
"Straight and Narrow"
Straight and narrow, we will choose,
If we do this, we can't lose.
He loves us and showed the way,
To live this value ev'ryday.

GOOD WORKS
"Let Our Light Shine"
Let our light shine ev'ryday,
Doing good works on our way.
He loves us and showed the way,
To live this value ev'ryday.

INTEGRITY
"Integrity"
Integrity leads our way,
In all we do and we say.
He loves us and showed the way,
To live this value ev'ryday.

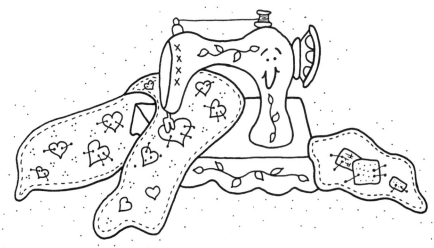

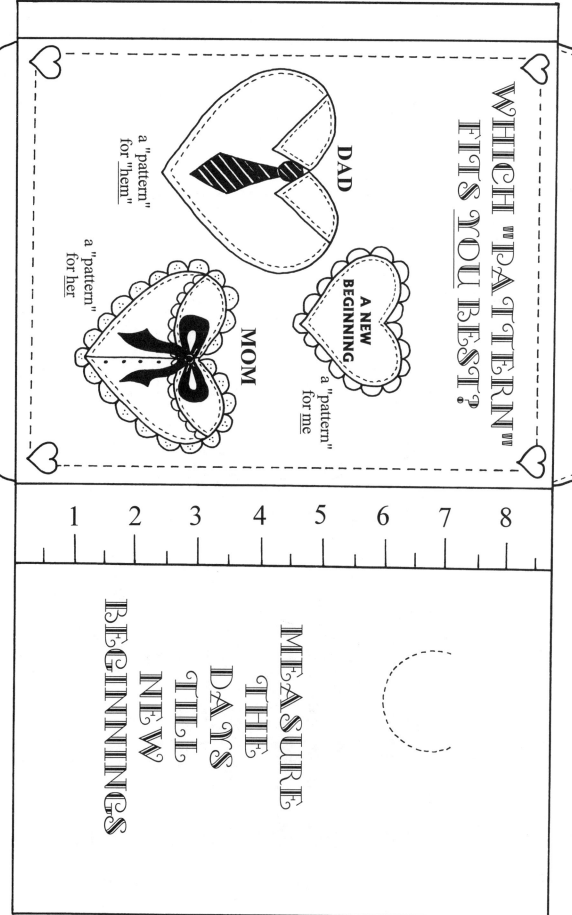

TO MAKE THE INVITATIONS:

Copy the invitation envelope, p. 13, onto white or ivory paper. Cut along the outside edges. Fold the left flap to the back along the black line. Fold the right flap to the back along the black line and glue it over the left flap to form the back of the envelope. Fold the bottom flap to the back and glue. Fold the top flap to the back. (Optional: Use colored pencils, felt pens or crayons to color the envelope.) Copy this page. Write or type your information on the heart. Copy onto pink paper. Cut the message and heart out along the outside border. Place a 1" strip of self-adhesive magnetic tape on the back of the heart. (The heart may be placed on each young woman's refrigerator for a reminder.) Insert one message and one heart into each envelope. Place a gold foil Young Woman sticker at the back of the envelope to seal the top flap closed.

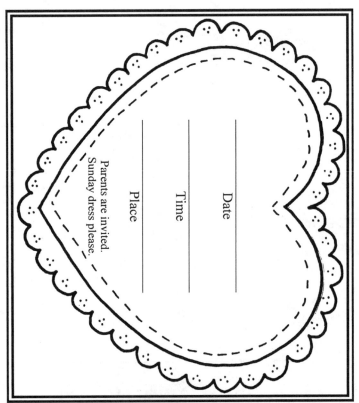

Date

Time

Place

Parents are invited.
Sunday dress please.

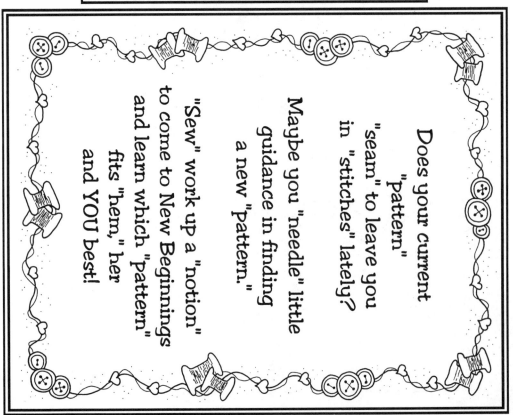

Does your current
"pattern"
"seam" to leave you
in "stitches" lately?

Maybe you "needle" little
guidance in finding
a new "pattern."

"Sew" work up a "notion"
to come to New Beginnings
and learn which "pattern"
fits "hem," her
and YOU best!

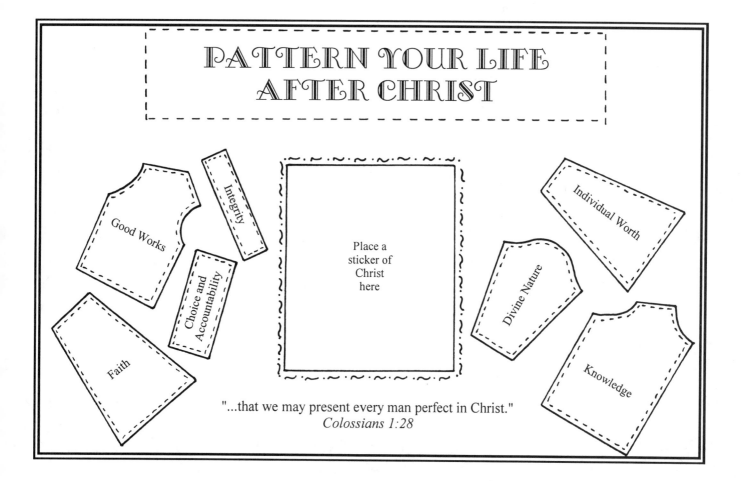

PATTERN YOUR LIFE
AFTER CHRIST

Integrity

Good Works

Choice and
Accountability

Faith

Place a
sticker of
Christ
here

Individual Worth

Divine Nature

Knowledge

"...that we may present every man perfect in Christ."
Colossians 1:28

TO MAKE THE HANDOUTS:

Copy the handout onto ivory paper. Cut along the outside edges. Fold the left flap to the back along the black line. Fold the right flap to the back along the black line and glue it over the left flap to form the back of the envelope. Fold the bottom flap to the back and glue. Fold the top flap to the back. Place a sticker of Christ where indicated. Copy the pattern pieces, pp. 18-24, onto the appropriate colored paper. Cut each pattern piece out. Place one pattern piece of each value into one envelope.

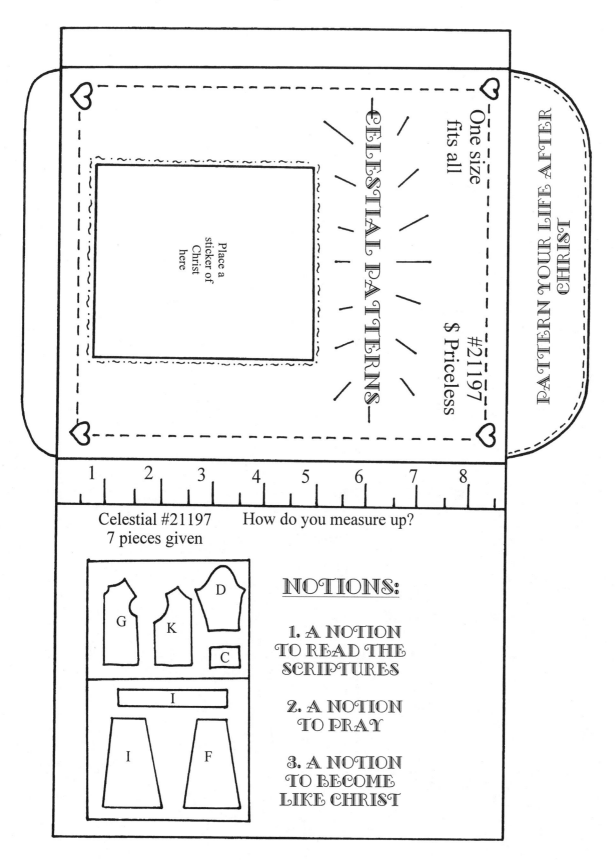

Place a sticker of Christ here

CELESTIAL PATTERNS

One size fits all

#21197
$ Priceless

PATTERN YOUR LIFE AFTER CHRIST

1 2 3 4 5 6 7 8

Celestial #21197   How do you measure up?
7 pieces given

G   K   D   C

I

I   F

NOTIONS:

1. A NOTION TO READ THE SCRIPTURES

2. A NOTION TO PRAY

3. A NOTION TO BECOME LIKE CHRIST

Copy onto white paper

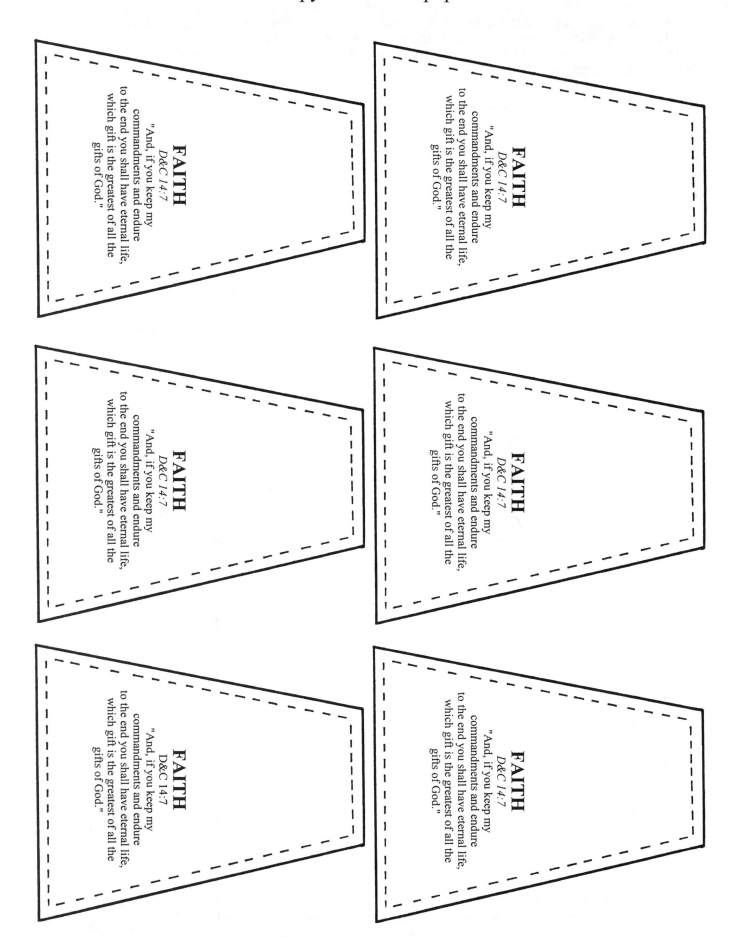

FAITH
D&C 14:7
"And, if you keep my
commandments and endure
to the end you shall have eternal life,
which gift is the greatest of all the
gifts of God."

FAITH
D&C 14:7
"And, if you keep my
commandments and endure
to the end you shall have eternal life,
which gift is the greatest of all the
gifts of God."

FAITH
D&C 14:7
"And, if you keep my
commandments and endure
to the end you shall have eternal life,
which gift is the greatest of all the
gifts of God."

FAITH
D&C 14:7
"And, if you keep my
commandments and endure
to the end you shall have eternal life,
which gift is the greatest of all the
gifts of God."

FAITH
D&C 14:7
"And, if you keep my
commandments and endure
to the end you shall have eternal life,
which gift is the greatest of all the
gifts of God."

FAITH
D&C 14:7
"And, if you keep my
commandments and endure
to the end you shall have eternal life,
which gift is the greatest of all the
gifts of God."

**DIVINE
NATURE**
2 Peter 1:4-7
"Be partakers of the divine nature,...
giving all diligence,
add to your faith virtue;
and to virtue knowledge;
And to knowledge temperance;
and to temperance patience;
and to patience godliness;
And to godliness brotherly kindness,
and to brotherly kindness charity."

**DIVINE
NATURE**
2 Peter 1:4-7
"Be partakers of the divine nature,...
giving all diligence,
add to your faith virtue;
and to virtue knowledge;
And to knowledge temperance;
and to temperance patience;
and to patience godliness;
And to godliness brotherly kindness,
and to brotherly kindness charity."

**DIVINE
NATURE**
2 Peter 1:4-7
"Be partakers of the divine nature,...
giving all diligence,
add to your faith virtue;
and to virtue knowledge;
And to knowledge temperance;
and to temperance patience;
and to patience godliness;
And to godliness brotherly kindness,
and to brotherly kindness charity."

**DIVINE
NATURE**
2 Peter 1:4-7
"Be partakers of the divine nature,...
giving all diligence,
add to your faith virtue;
and to virtue knowledge;
And to knowledge temperance;
and to temperance patience;
and to patience godliness;
And to godliness brotherly kindness,
and to brotherly kindness charity."

Copy onto red paper

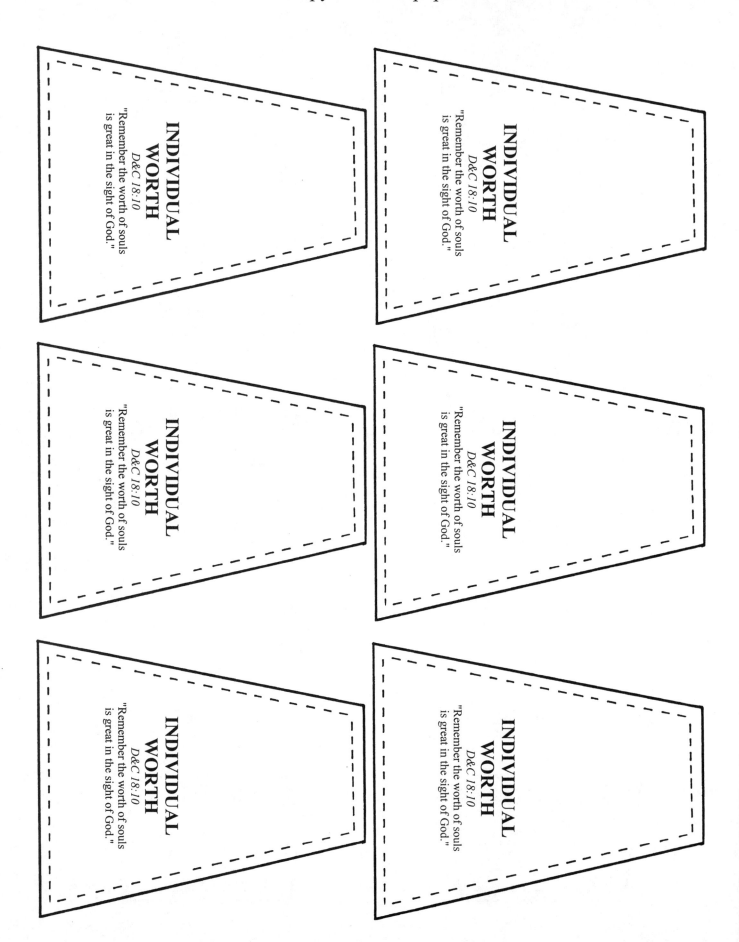

INDIVIDUAL WORTH
D&C 18:10
"Remember the worth of souls is great in the sight of God."

INDIVIDUAL WORTH
D&C 18:10
"Remember the worth of souls is great in the sight of God."

INDIVIDUAL WORTH
D&C 18:10
"Remember the worth of souls is great in the sight of God."

INDIVIDUAL WORTH
D&C 18:10
"Remember the worth of souls is great in the sight of God."

INDIVIDUAL WORTH
D&C 18:10
"Remember the worth of souls is great in the sight of God."

INDIVIDUAL WORTH
D&C 18:10
"Remember the worth of souls is great in the sight of God."

-3-

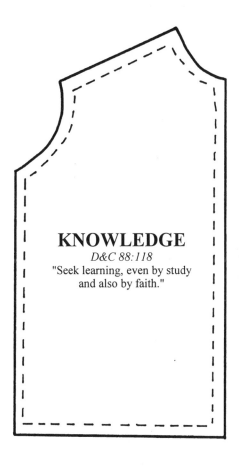

KNOWLEDGE
D&C 88:118
"Seek learning, even by study
and also by faith."

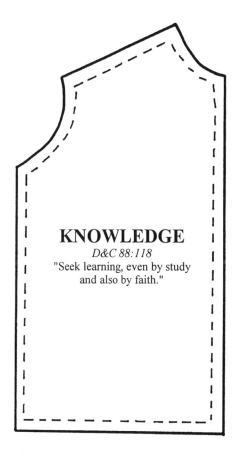

KNOWLEDGE
D&C 88:118
"Seek learning, even by study
and also by faith."

KNOWLEDGE
D&C 88:118
"Seek learning, even by study
and also by faith."

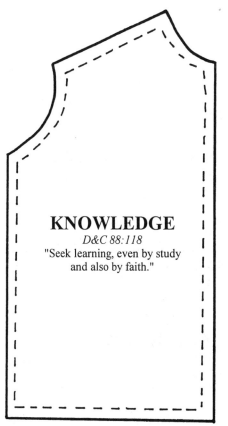

KNOWLEDGE
D&C 88:118
"Seek learning, even by study
and also by faith."

Copy onto orange paper

**CHOICE AND
ACCOUNTABILITY**
Joshua 24:15
"Choose you this day whom ye will serve...
but as for me and my house, we will serve the Lord."

**CHOICE AND
ACCOUNTABILITY**
Joshua 24:15
"Choose you this day whom ye will serve...
but as for me and my house, we will serve the Lord."

**CHOICE AND
ACCOUNTABILITY**
Joshua 24:15
"Choose you this day whom ye will serve...
but as for me and my house, we will serve the Lord."

**CHOICE AND
ACCOUNTABILITY**
Joshua 24:15
"Choose you this day whom ye will serve...
but as for me and my house, we will serve the Lord."

**CHOICE AND
ACCOUNTABILITY**
Joshua 24:15
"Choose you this day whom ye will serve...
but as for me and my house, we will serve the Lord."

**CHOICE AND
ACCOUNTABILITY**
Joshua 24:15
"Choose you this day whom ye will serve...
but as for me and my house, we will serve the Lord."

**CHOICE AND
ACCOUNTABILITY**
Joshua 24:15
"Choose you this day whom ye will serve...
but as for me and my house, we will serve the Lord."

**CHOICE AND
ACCOUNTABILITY**
Joshua 24:15
"Choose you this day whom ye will serve...
but as for me and my house, we will serve the Lord."

**CHOICE AND
ACCOUNTABILITY**
Joshua 24:15
"Choose you this day whom ye will serve...
but as for me and my house, we will serve the Lord."

**CHOICE AND
ACCOUNTABILITY**
Joshua 24:15
"Choose you this day whom ye will serve...
but as for me and my house, we will serve the Lord."

Copy onto yellow paper

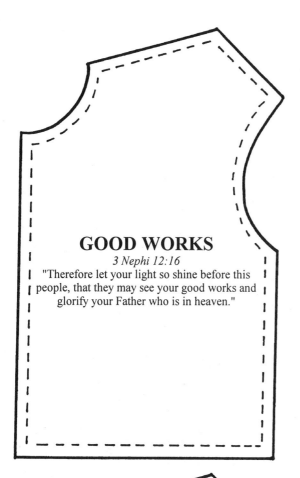

GOOD WORKS
3 Nephi 12:16
"Therefore let your light so shine before this people, that they may see your good works and glorify your Father who is in heaven."

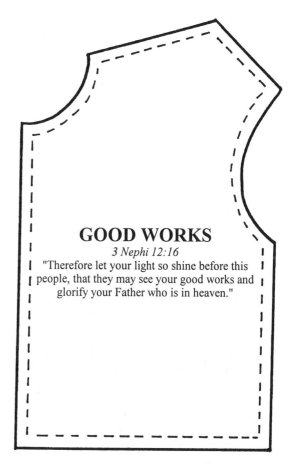

GOOD WORKS
3 Nephi 12:16
"Therefore let your light so shine before this people, that they may see your good works and glorify your Father who is in heaven."

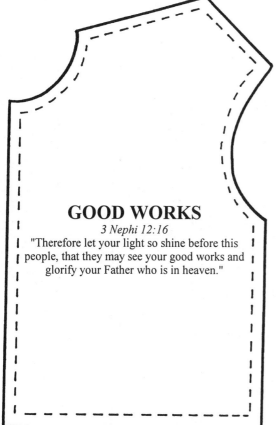

GOOD WORKS
3 Nephi 12:16
"Therefore let your light so shine before this people, that they may see your good works and glorify your Father who is in heaven."

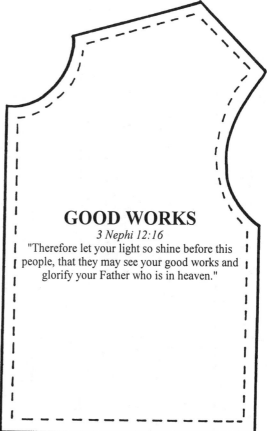

GOOD WORKS
3 Nephi 12:16
"Therefore let your light so shine before this people, that they may see your good works and glorify your Father who is in heaven."

one

Copy onto purple paper

INTEGRITY

Job 27:5

"Till I die I will not remove mine integrity from me."

INTEGRITY

Job 27:5

"Till I die I will not remove mine integrity from me."

INTEGRITY

Job 27:5

"Till I die I will not remove mine integrity from me."

INTEGRITY

Job 27:5

"Till I die I will not remove mine integrity from me."

INTEGRITY

Job 27:5

"Till I die I will not remove mine integrity from me."

INTEGRITY

Job 27:5

"Till I die I will not remove mine integrity from me."

INTEGRITY

Job 27:5

"Till I die I will not remove mine integrity from me."

INTEGRITY

Job 27:5

"Till I die I will not remove mine integrity from me."

INTEGRITY

Job 27:5

"Till I die I will not remove mine integrity from me."

INTEGRITY

Job 27:5

"Till I die I will not remove mine integrity from me."

One size
fits all

#21197
$ Priceless

CELESTIAL PATTERNS

PATTERN YOUR LIFE AFTER CHRIST

Glue a
picture of
Christ
here

"...that we may present every man perfect in Christ."
Colossians 1:28

FAITH

"FORM" your life around faith

DIVINE NATURE

Your nature is "SEW" divine!

INDIVIDUAL WORTH

You have "IMMEASURABLE" worth!

KNOWLEDGE

"THREAD" your mind with knowledge

CHOICE
AND
ACCOUNTABILITY

Be sure to make wise choices and
"STICK" with them

GOOD WORKS

The Lord may "NEEDLE" little help from you in serving others

INTEGRITY

"STITCH" integrity into your actions

"Picture This... An Eternal Marriage"

"For if you will that I give unto you a place in the celestial world, you must prepare yourselves by doing the things which I have commanded you and required of you." *D&C 78:7*

OBJECTIVE:

To encourage each young woman to be preparing for a temple marriage now and to provide a spiritual evening for her to spend with her mother.

MATERIALS NEEDED:

An invitation for each young woman to be invited, see p. 40

A program for everyone to be invited, see pp. 41-42

A handout for each young woman to be invited, see pp. 43-44

A copy of "The Wedding Bouquet" skit for the director and each participant, pp. 35-39

A spotlight, props and costumes for the skit

PREPARATION:

1. Make the assignments using the suggested Program Outline/Assignment Sheet, p. 34.
2. Assign the parts for the skit.
3. Schedule practice times for the skit, including a dress rehearsal.
4. Assign the speaker.
5. Talk with the mothers of the young women before the event and invite them to wear their appropriate wedding dresses.
6. Schedule the church building for the evening of the event, allowing enough time to set up and decorate the afternoon of the event.

SUGGESTIONS FOR DECORATIONS:

1. Hang pictures of temples on the walls. If possible, obtain temple wedding pictures of the young women's parents to hang on the walls.
2. Decorate the refreshment table in white (to simulate a wedding reception) using a white tablecloth, white bouquet of flowers, etc.

SUGGESTIONS FOR REFRESHMENTS:

Wedding cake, nuts, mints and punch to drink (to simulate a wedding reception).

_____Opening song: "Families Can Be Together Forever," hymnbook, p. 300

_____Opening prayer

_____Welcome: Include the objective of the program.

_____Presentation of "The Wedding Bouquet" skit

_____Speaker: Be sure to include these points:
  *If we have faith in the Lord's eternal plan, we will desire a temple marriage. If we lack that faith, then we need to seek for it through prayer, scripture study, etc.
  *A temple marriage is necessary to achieve the highest degree of the celestial kingdom.
  *Now is the time to prepare for a temple marriage in the future.

_____Closing remarks: Distribute the "Picture This" and/or the "Rose" handouts.

_____Closing song: "Dearest Children, God Is Near You," hymnbook, p. 96

_____Closing prayer and blessing on the refreshments

_____Refreshments: (allow a short time for visiting)
  Wedding cake, nuts, mints and punch to drink

More Assignments to Consider

_____Preparation of invitations	_____Refreshments organizer
_____Preparation of programs	_____Decorations organizer
_____Preparation of handouts	_____Setup organizer
_____Skit director/organizer	_____Cleanup organizer

INSTRUCTIONS FOR MAKING THE INVITATIONS, PROGRAMS AND HANDOUTS

INVITATIONS: Make a copy of the invitation (p. 40). Write or type your information on the invitation. Copy this onto white paper. Fold in half and then in half again with the large temple on the front. Optional: Lightly spray each invitation with iridescent glitter. Distribute one to each young woman one week prior to the event.

PROGRAMS: Make a copy of the program border (p. 42). Write or type your program information inside the border. Copy the program front (p. 41) onto white paper with the border on the reverse side of the paper. Fold in half.

HANDOUTS: Two handout ideas are supplied. *Rose:* Copy the rose handouts (p. 43) onto white paper. Cut out along the outside border. Use a hole punch to make a hole in the upper left corner. Use white ribbon to attach each one to a fresh or silk white rose. *Picture This:* Copy the picture handout (p. 44) onto heavy white paper. Cut along the outside border. Glue to lightweight cardboard. Glue white lace around the outside edge. Attach a white ribbon for a hanger. Lightly spray with iridescent glitter.

"The Wedding Bouquet"
Eternal Marriage Skit

PLAYERS:

Sarah - a girl or young woman appropriate for each age: age 3, age 7, age 12, age 16 and age 21
Dad - a man of appropriate age to have a 21-year-old daughter
Sister Hill - a woman
Brother Smith - a man
Sister Wilson - a woman
Sister Taylor - a woman
Husband-to-be - a young man old enough to be a returned missionary
Two other children of each age: age 3, age 7, age 12 and age 16

SETTINGS:

You will be switching back and forth between these two settings throughout the skit.

Setting 1 - Spotlight on Sarah (age 21) dressed in a wedding dress and holding a wedding bouquet containing four white roses. Standing next to Sarah is her father dressed in a white suit. It is apparent that they are about to enter the temple for her wedding. (If you are an artist, a large drawing of a temple would make a great background scenery. Or make a transparency of a temple and project it onto a white wall with a spotlight on Sarah and her dad standing off to the side of the temple.)

Setting 2 - A classroom set up with three chairs for children and a chair for the teacher. Use this classroom throughout the skit, changing the people according to the script.

SARAH:

I can't believe it's actually my wedding day. I've planned for this day all my life.

DAD:

You look beautiful, Sarah. I'm very proud of you and your choice to marry in the temple. I have something for you. *(He hands her a white rose.)* A white rose to add to your wedding bouquet.

SARAH:

It's perfect. Thank you, Dad. Each rose in my bouquet represents something I've learned that has helped me prepare for my temple marriage. *(She points to a rose in her bouquet.)* I remember the first rose I received for my bouquet. I was barely in Primary and Sister Hill was my teacher. She was giving a lesson on.....

The spotlight moves to Setting 2, which shows Sarah, age 3, two other 3-year-olds and Sister Hill.

SISTER HILL:

Heavenly Father is actually the father of your spirit. Just as your dad here on earth loves you, your Father in Heaven also loves you and so does Jesus. If you have faith that Heavenly Father loves you and you are his child, then you'll always try to do what he wants you to do.

SARAH:
I know that I am a child of God. *(She sings, "I Am a Child of God," hymnbook, p. 301.)*

SISTER HILL:
That was beautiful, Sarah. I can see that you have great faith in your Heavenly Father and in Jesus. I want to give you this white rose to remind you of the faith that you now have. *(She hands Sarah a white rose.)*

SARAH:
Thank you, Sister Hill.

The spotlight returns to Setting 1.

DAD:
You've always had faith in your Heavenly Father, Sarah, even when things were getting tough in your life. *(He points to another rose in the bouquet.)* What about this rose? When did you receive it?

SARAH:
Let's see... Oh, I remember. I was about seven years old and still in Primary. Brother Smith was teaching about....

The spotlight moves to Setting 2, which shows Sarah, age 7, two other 7-year-olds and Brother Smith.

BROTHER SMITH:
1 Nephi 22:31 says, "Wherefore, if ye shall be obedient to the commandments, and endure to the end, ye shall be saved at the last day." What are some of the commandments the Lord has given us?

1ST 7-YEAR-OLD:
He said we should go to church and pray.

BROTHER SMITH:
That's right. Any other commandments you can think of?

2ND 7-YEAR-OLD:
We should pay our tithing and obey our parents.

BROTHER SMITH:
Those all are good examples.

SARAH:
What happens if I don't keep every commandment all the time, even though I try to?

BROTHER SMITH:

Nobody is perfect and the Lord knows this. He gives us the opportunity to repent and if we do, then he forgives us. He wants us to succeed. He gives us commandments so we can be better people and more like him. I'm giving you this white rose to remind you to keep the commandments and to repent when you need to. *(He hands Sarah a white rose.)*

SARAH:

Thank you, Brother Smith. *(She sings, "Keep the Commandments," hymnbook, p. 303)*

The spotlight returns to Setting 1.

SARAH:

(pointing to the rose) This rose has reminded me to keep the commandments. I've done my best and I've repented often.

DAD:

You've been a good example to all of your family, including me.

SARAH:

Now this rose *(points to another rose in her bouquet)*, I remember well. I had just entered Young Women and Sister Wilson was teaching us about temples....

The spotlight moves to setting 2, which shows Sarah, age 12, two other 12-year-olds and Sister Wilson.

SISTER WILSON:

Today we are going to learn about temples. What can you tell me about the temple?

1ST 12-YEAR-OLD:

It's a sacred place.

SISTER WILSON:

That's right, but did you know that our bodies are temples also? This means that our bodies are sacred places. Would we want any unclean thing to enter the temple?

ALL GIRLS:

No.

SISTER WILSON:

Our bodies are our own personal temples and we should keep them clean. We feel better physically and spiritually about ourselves when we are clean. What are some ways we can do this?

2ND 12-YEAR-OLD:
We can keep the Word of Wisdom by not drinking or smoking and making sure to get enough exercise.

SARAH:
We can follow the prophets' counsel to not date until we're sixteen. We can wear modest clothing.

SISTER WILSON:
These are all ways for us to keep our temple bodies clean and sacred.

SARAH:
(She sings, "The Lord Gave Me a Temple," Children's Songbook, p. 153.)

SISTER WILSON:
(She hands Sarah a white rose.) I have a white rose for you, Sarah. I want it to remind you to keep your temple clean.

SARAH:
Thank you, Sister Wilson.

The spotlight returns to Setting 1.

DAD:
You've kept your temple clean, Sarah. You are as unspotted and white as the rose you received that day.

SARAH:
(She points to another rose in her bouquet.) I was a Laurel when I received this rose. We had many lessons about the importance of temple marriage. In fact, the Laurel motto is .....

The spotlight moves to Setting 2, which shows Sarah, age 16, two other 16-year-old girls and Sister Taylor.

SISTER TAYLOR:
Who can tell me what the Laurel motto is?

1ST 16-YEAR-OLD:
"The temple spires remind us of sacred ordinances and covenants that lead to exaltation."

SISTER TAYLOR:
We need a temple marriage to receive these ordinances and to live with our family and Heavenly Father in eternal life.

2ND 16-YEAR-OLD:

Why do we have so many lessons about temple marriage? We're not even looking to get married yet.

SISTER TAYLOR:

I know you don't want to be married yet, but you can't just go to the temple when you decide to be married; you need to prepare. Now is the time for each of you to be preparing for a temple marriage. You need to be practicing worthy dating habits, dating worthy boys and wearing modest clothing. You also need to prepare yourselves spiritually by reading the scriptures, praying and obeying the commandments.

SARAH:

I've been preparing my whole life. But now, as I get older, I know I need to make the extra effort to prepare for my temple wedding. *(She sings, "I Love to See the Temple,"* Children's Songbook, *p. 95)*

SISTER TAYLOR:

(She hands Sarah a white rose.) Sarah, I hope this pure white rose will remind you of the necessary preparation you will need for a temple marriage.

SARAH:

Thank you, Sister Taylor.

The spotlight returns to Setting 1.

SARAH:

(She holds up the rose her dad gave her.) Now, with this rose from you, Dad, my wedding bouquet is complete.

DAD:

This rose has a meaning also, Sarah. I've watched you grow physically and spiritually. I am so proud of you. I want this rose to remind you to endure to the end. Keep adding roses to your bouquet of spiritual growth. Always look to your Father in Heaven for guidance. *(He sings, "Walk Tall, You're a Daughter of God.")*

Sarah hugs her father. Her husband-to-be walks up to her and holds his hand out to her. She reaches her hand out to him. Turn the spotlight off.

You and your mom are invited to a very special program.

Date: _____

Time: _____

Place: _____

Church dress please
Refreshments will be served

*Picture this
for your wedding day...*

*an eternal marriage,
the Lord's way.*

Picture This... An Eternal Marriage

Picture this rose
as a virtue
you've earned
along the way.
And strive to
gather more roses,
to add to your
wedding bouquet.

Picture this rose
as a virtue
you've earned
along the way.
And strive to
gather more roses,
to add to your
wedding bouquet.

Picture this rose
as a virtue
you've earned
along the way.
And strive to
gather more roses,
to add to your
wedding bouquet.

Picture this rose
as a virtue
you've earned
along the way.
And strive to
gather more roses,
to add to your
wedding bouquet.

Picture this temple
As you live each day,
Make the right choices
That will lead you this way.

Picture this temple
As you begin to date.
Is the young man you're with
Worthy of a temple mate?

Picture this temple
As your wedding you plan.
For you'll want to spend eternity
With this young man.

Now enter this temple
On your special day,
Knowing you've lived worthy,
You've lived the Lord's way.

DIVINE NATURE

"The Royal Ball"

"That ye would walk worthy of God, who hath called you unto his kingdom and glory."
1 Thessalonians 2:12

OBJECTIVE:

To help each young woman realize she is divine because she is a daughter of Heavenly Father and that she should always act in accordance to his will. Also to provide an elegant evening for her to attend a dance with her escort (father, uncle, home teacher, etc.).

MATERIALS NEEDED:

An invitation for each young woman to be invited, see p. 47
A program for everyone to be invited, see pp. 49-50
A handout for each young woman to be invited, see p. 48

PREPARATION:

1. Make the assignments using the suggested Program Outline/Assignment Sheet, p. 46.
2. Assign the speaker.
3. Assign an escort to sing "Walk Tall, You're a Daughter of God" during "The Royal Decree" presentation, see p. 46.
4. Assign a couple to teach a simple ballroom dance.
5. Schedule the church building for the evening of the event, allowing enough time to set up and decorate the afternoon of the event.

SUGGESTIONS FOR DECORATIONS:

1. Use a royal blue tablecloth for the refreshment table. Swag silver garland along the table with silver metallic paper ribbon bows.
2. Incorporate silver stars throughout to remind the young women that their court is in heaven. (Hang stars on the walls, scatter star confetti on the table, etc.)
3. Roll out a white paper runner for the girls to walk up to receive their "Royal Decree."
4. Be sure to set out chairs to provide an opportunity for the guests to sit down during the speaker and dance.

SUGGESTIONS FOR REFRESHMENTS:

Cheesecake with cherry topping and punch to drink. (Try to make it elegant.)

"The Royal Ball"
Program Outline and Assignment Sheet

_____Opening song: "O My Father," hymnbook, p. 292

_____Opening prayer

_____Welcome: Include the objective of the program.

_____Speaker: Be sure to include these points:
        *We are Heavenly Father's daughters. That makes us princesses.
        *We should act worthy of God's kingdom at all times.

_____Dance instruction: Prearrange to have a simple ballroom dance taught.

_____Dance

_____Presentation of "The Royal Decree" handouts
        *Prearrange to have one of the escorts sing, "Walk Tall, You're a
        Daughter of God" as each young woman walks up to receive
        her copy of the decree.

_____Closing Remarks: Be sure to compliment the young women for acting like
        princesses throughout the night.

_____Closing song: "I Know My Father Lives," hymnbook, p. 302

_____Closing prayer and blessing on the refreshments

_____Refreshments: Cheesecake with cherry topping and punch to drink

More Assignments to Consider

_____Preparation of invitations   _____Decorations organizer
_____Preparation of programs   _____Setup organizer
_____Preparation of handouts   _____Cleanup organizer
_____Refreshments organizer

INSTRUCTIONS FOR MAKING THE INVITATIONS, PROGRAMS AND HANDOUTS

INVITATIONS: Make a copy of the invitation (p. 47). Write or type your information on the invitation. Copy this onto blue paper. Write a young woman's name on each one. Roll up (like a scroll) and tie with gold elastic cording. One week prior to the event, deliver an invitation to each young woman's house and say, "I am a messenger of the royal court, and I have an official invitation for you."

PROGRAMS: Make a copy of the program border (p. 50). Write or type your program information inside the border. Copy the program front (p. 49) onto blue paper with the border on the reverse side of the paper. Fold in half.

HANDOUTS: _The Royal Decree:_ Copy the decree (p. 48) onto blue paper. Roll up (like a scroll) and tie with gold elastic cording.

The royal court requests
the presence of
Princess _____
and her escort
at the
"Royal Ball"

Date: _____

Time: _____

Place: _____

Please dress in your best church clothes
Refreshments will be served

The Royal Decree

Hear ye, hear ye,
Young woman of royal birth,
As a daughter of Heavenly Father,
Know that you have divine worth.

A princess you are,
An heir to his kingdom.
Always remember your heritage
And where you have come from.

Be sure to present yourself,
A princess with noble means,
Whether in a ball gown and jewels
Or in a ball cap and jeans.

Work to live your life
In such a divine way
That you may inherit the blessings
Heavenly Father promised you can have someday.

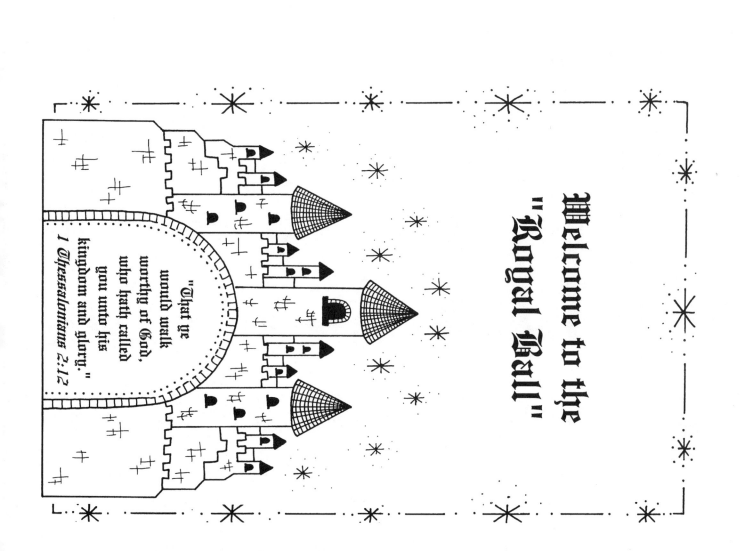

"That ye
would walk
worthy of God,
who hath called
you unto his
kingdom and glory."
1 Thessalonians 2:12

Welcome to the
"Royal Ball"

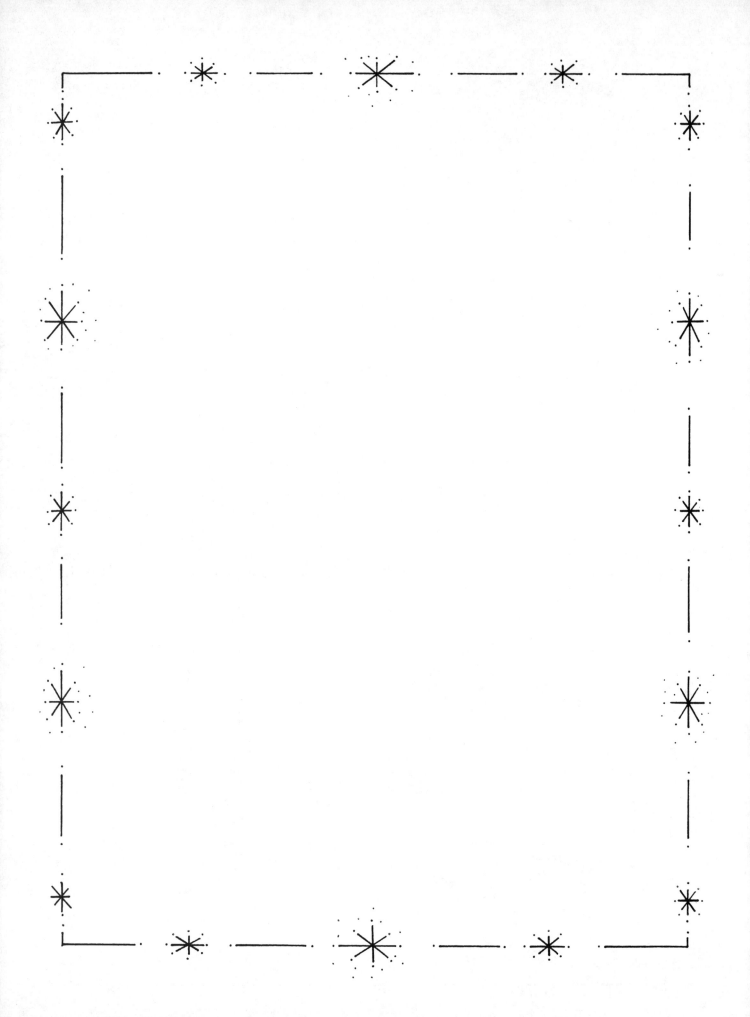

"RALLY TOGETHER"

"...that every man may improve upon his talent, that every man may gain other talents...
to become the common property of the whole church." *D&C 82:18*

OBJECTIVE:

To help each young woman realize she has talents and qualities that are unique to her and that she can benefit herself and others by sharing those talents. Also to provide her with a fun opportunity to use her talents while working within a team consisting of young women and young men.

MATERIALS NEEDED:

An invitation for everyone to be invited, see p. 55
A program for everyone to be invited, see pp. 57-58
A handout for everyone to be invited, see p. 56
Any items needed for the "Rally Together" activity, see pp. 53-54

PREPARATION:

1. Arrange for support and help with this program from the Young Men presidency.
2. Make the assignments using the suggested Program Outline/Assignment Sheet, p. 52.
3. Assign the speaker.
4. Schedule the church building for the evening of the event, allowing enough time to set up and decorate the afternoon of the event.

SUGGESTIONS FOR DECORATIONS:

1. Use a black or white tablecloth on the refreshment table. Outline the table with a purchased black and white checkered flag garland. Place small model cars on the table.
2. Copy the road signs, pp. 59-67, onto the appropriate colored paper. Cut them out and hang them on the wall above the refreshment table.

SUGGESTIONS FOR REFRESHMENTS:

Rocky road ice cream with sugar cookies. (Use a car-shaped cookie cutter if you can find one, or cut the cookies into the shape of road signs.)

"RALLY TOGETHER"
Program Outline and Assignment Sheet

_____Opening song: "Every Star Is Different," *Children's Songbook,* p. 142

_____Opening prayer

_____Welcome: Include the objective of the program.

_____Speaker: Be sure to include these points:
> *Each of us has unique talents and qualities.
> *We have talents that are yet undiscovered and we need to be actively seeking them.
> *We need to share these talents with others.

_____"Rally Together" activity, see pp. 53-54

_____Closing remarks: Distribute the "Rally Together" handouts

_____Closing song: "Lead Me into Life Eternal," hymnbook, p. 45

_____Closing prayer and blessing on the refreshments

_____Refreshments: Rocky road ice cream and sugar cookies

More Assignments to Consider

_____Preparation of invitations _____Refreshments organizer
_____Preparation of programs _____Setup organizer
_____Preparation of handouts _____Cleanup organizer
_____"Rally Together" activity organizer

INSTRUCTIONS FOR MAKING THE INVITATIONS, PROGRAMS AND HANDOUTS

INVITATIONS: Make a copy of the invitation (p. 55). Write or type your information on the invitation. Copy this onto red paper. Distribute one to each young woman and young man one week prior to the event.

PROGRAMS: Make a copy of the program border (p. 58). Write or type your program information inside the border. Copy the program front (p. 57) onto red paper with the border on the reverse side of the paper. Fold in half.

HANDOUTS: *Rally Together:* Copy the handouts (p. 56) onto red paper. Cut each one out along the outside border. (Optional: Hot glue or tape a small plastic purchased car to each handout.)

need @ least 8 adults
Bro & Sis Varty
Bro Svenson
Bro & Sis Robinson
Bro. Holman or Kinney
Bro Sheridan + Sis (??)

"RALLY TOGETHER"
Activity Preparation and Outline

PREPARATION FOR THE ACTIVITY

1. **Gather supplies to make the cars.**
   very large cardboard boxes
   colored construction paper
   colored marking pens
   (any items that may be used to decorate the boxes)
   box knives, scissors, glue, tape

   For each car: Cut away the top and bottom flaps from a cardboard box. Decorate the box with marking pens, colored paper, etc., to create a "car." For example: Glue four large black construction paper circles to each side of the "car" for tires and glue two white construction paper circles to the front of the "car" for headlights. The team members will step into their "cars" and hold them up around their bodies with their hands while they travel. Each team will need to make enough cars for everyone to fit (more than one team member should be able to fit into the large boxes).

2. **Copy the road signs, pp. 59-67, onto the appropriate colored paper.**
   Each sign will be hung at the appropriate station.
   STOP/YIELD - red paper
   REST AREA - blue paper
   SCHOOL CROSSING/CATTLE CROSSING - yellow paper
   DETOUR - orange paper
   ONE WAY/ROAD BLOCK/FINISH LINE - white paper

3. **Gather items needed for each station.**
   Refer to each station road sign for setting up each station. For example: At the REST AREA STATION you may have a table set up like a lemonade stand. After the team member sings the Primary song, give him/her a glass of lemonade.

4. **Assign adult leaders or parents to be station monitors.**
   Assign a station monitor for each station. Refer to each station road sign, pp. 59-67, to assign any other participants you may need. For example: You will need to use a young girl for the SCHOOL CROSSING STATION.

5. **Decide where each station will be located in the building.**
   Make up different routes for each team to follow. Starting teams at different areas and having them follow different routes will help reduce "traffic jams." All teams should end up at the finish line.

OUTLINE FOR THE ACTIVITY

1. **Divide into teams.**

   Divide the youth into teams with four or five youth on each team. Each team should consist of both young women and young men. Try to put youth with different talents, abilities and age levels together. The object is for each member to contribute a different talent that will help enable the entire team to reach the finish line (celestial kingdom).

2. **Make the cars.**

   Allow time for each team to make their car(s) (see p. 53).

3. **Explain the objective and rules of the game.**

   Explain to each team that it is a journey to the celestial kingdom. This is not a timed race and there will not be just one winner. The idea is for all teams to be winners. As team members make their journey, they will come across obstacles or challenges that may slow them down. At each obstacle (station) they will be required to do something. At each station, one team member will be allowed to leave the car to do what is required at that station. It will be up to the station monitor to decide if they have successfully accomplished the task and to allow the whole team to pass through. They should take turns throughout the journey allowing each team member one or two chances to use their talents. Every team member should participate at least once, if possible.

4. **Hand out the travel routes.**

   Give each team a route explaining what order they should travel to each station.

5. **Activity.**

   Allow time for each team to finish the journey.

6. **Finish line.**

   You may want to have the finish line end up near the refreshment table. This will put everyone back together for the closing remarks and refreshments.

7. **Closing remarks.**

   Be sure to emphasize to the youth how impressed you were with them during the activity. Stress to them how great it was to see their willingness to share their talents as they worked together as a team.

RALLY TOGETHER, YOU AND ME, ON OUR WAY TO ETERNITY!

"RALLY TOGETHER"
AND SHARE YOUR TALENTS
ALONG THE ROAD TO ETERNITY!

"RALLY TOGETHER"
AND SHARE YOUR TALENTS
ALONG THE ROAD TO ETERNITY!

"RALLY TOGETHER"
AND SHARE YOUR TALENTS
ALONG THE ROAD TO ETERNITY!

"RALLY TOGETHER"
AND SHARE YOUR TALENTS
ALONG THE ROAD TO ETERNITY!

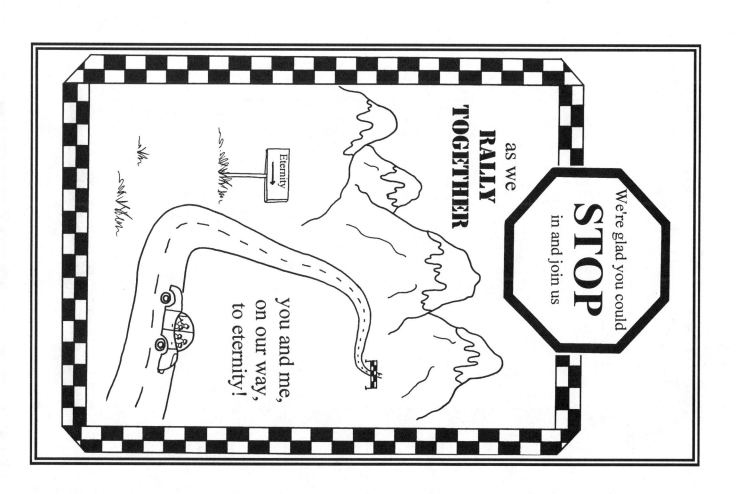

As you stop for the detour, a stranded motorist waves you down. He is having car problems. Do you think you can help him? It may be anything from a flat tire to a bad water pump. Ask him for the symptoms of the problem and then try to decide what is wrong with the car. Explain to him how to fix the problem.

YOU MUST DECIDE WHAT IS WRONG WITH THE STRANDED MOTORIST'S CAR AND TELL HIM HOW TO FIX IT. WHEN THE STATION MONITOR IS SATISFIED, YOU MAY CONTINUE ON YOUR JOURNEY.

Here you are at a cattle crossing. A whole herd of cattle have just crossed, but unfortunately for you, one has decided to take a nap in the middle of the road. It is completely blocking your way. You honk, but it still doesn't move. How do you get it to move without harming it or anyone else? Use your imagination!

YOU MUST FIND A WAY TO GET THE COW TO MOVE OUT OF THE ROAD. WHEN THE STATION MONITOR IS SATISFIED, YOU MAY CONTINUE ON YOUR JOURNEY.

"Why must I yield here?" you ask the station monitor.
The station monitor answers, "Because I love sports and I want
you to tell me about the last sports game you played."
Tell details about the game. For example: What was the score?
What position did you play? Was it a school game or something
else? Were you happy with the way you played? etc.

**YOU MUST TELL DETAILS ABOUT YOUR
LAST SPORTS GAME. WHEN THE STATION
MONITOR IS SATISFIED, YOU MAY
CONTINUE ON YOUR JOURNEY.**

Here you are, stuck at a road block. The construction worker tells you it may be hours until he can let you pass through. "However," he says, "I do have some paper and a pencil. Why don't you draw me a picture to pass the time more quickly." So draw the picture and by the time you're finished, it may be time to pass through the road block.

YOU MUST DRAW A PICTURE TO PASS THE TIME AT THE ROAD BLOCK. WHEN THE STATION MONITOR IS SATISFIED, YOU MAY CONTINUE ON YOUR JOURNEY.

What's going on? You see a construction worker holding up a
one-way sign but the road is two-way. You ask about it.
The road worker says, "There's only one way I'll let you pass.
If you recite a poem, I'll let you continue on your journey!"
It can be an existing poem or you can make one up,
but it must have at least four lines.
Here is an example:
This game is fun,
And I'm happy to play,
But I'll be glad when it's done,
And I can be on my way!

**YOU MUST RECITE A POEM. WHEN THE
STATION MONITOR IS SATISFIED, YOU
MAY CONTINUE ON YOUR JOURNEY.**

You've come to a school crossing. You notice a young girl standing by the side of the road. She is crying. You ask her, "What is wrong?" She tells you, "I missed story time today at school." Tell her a short story (1 - 2 minutes) that will cheer her up. It can be an existing story or you can make one up.

YOU MUST TELL THE YOUNG GIRL A SHORT STORY TO CHEER HER UP. WHEN THE STATION MONITOR IS SATISFIED, YOU MAY CONTINUE ON YOUR JOURNEY.

You've stopped at the rest area. You are very thirsty and someone at the rest area tells you, "There is nowhere to stop for a drink for miles and miles!" You are having good luck, as there is a lemonade stand set up at the rest area. You must have a glass of lemonade before you leave this station. The problem is that the lemonade vendor doesn't take money. Instead you must sing one verse of a Primary song for your glass of lemonade.

YOU MUST SING A PRIMARY SONG. WHEN THE STATION MONITOR IS SATISFIED, YOU MAY CONTINUE ON YOUR JOURNEY.

As you stop at this stop sign, you notice a diner. It's just about mealtime and you're very hungry. You go to the diner to eat. The waitress informs you that you must play some music for your meal. Remember, music can be made with many different types of instruments. You may use spoons, snap your fingers, etc. Use your imagination and be creative.

YOU MUST PLAY MUSIC FOR YOUR MEAL. WHEN THE STATION MONITOR IS SATISFIED, YOU MAY CONTINUE ON YOUR JOURNEY.

CONGRATULATIONS!

Your talents, creativity and teamwork have brought you to the finish line of this journey. This was just a game and, of course, in real life you are still on your journey to the celestial kingdom. Always try to use your talents to help others as you rally together along the road to eternity.

CONGRATULATIONS ON YOUR TEAMWORK AND FOR SHARING YOUR OWN INDIVIDUAL TALENTS. YOU MAY NOW CROSS THE FINISH LINE INTO THE CELESTIAL KINGDOM.

"SUPER SATURDAY IN SPRING"

"O, remember... and learn wisdom in thy youth..." Alma 37:35

OBJECTIVE:

To help each young woman realize the importance of gaining knowledge in all areas and to provide her with a full day of hands-on experience learning new skills.

MATERIALS NEEDED:

An invitation for everyone to be invited, see p. 72

A program for everyone to be invited, see pp. 73-74

Any items needed for classes (This will depend on what classes you choose. See pp. 70-71)

(It is not necessary to provide a handout for this event because each young woman will be taking home the items she makes in her classes.)

PREPARATION:

1. Make the assignments using the suggested Program Outline/Assignment Sheet, p. 69.
2. Decide on classes from pp. 70-71, or use your own ideas. Classes should be low in cost. Find teachers for each class.
3. Schedule the church building for the day of the event, allowing for setup time that morning or the evening before.
4. Assign the speaker.
5. Talk to your bishop about the best way to finance this event. You may want to ask each girl to bring money for each class she takes or finance it through the ward budget.

SUGGESTIONS FOR DECORATIONS:

1. Use pastel-colored tablecloths on the tables with a potted flower for each centerpiece.
2. Copy border from p. 74 onto pastel-colored paper and use as place mats for table settings.
3. Copy border from p. 74 onto pastel-colored paper, write the class names on them and hang on the classroom doors to designate each class location.

SUGGESTIONS FOR DRINK AND DESSERT:

Provide punch for each girl to drink with her sack lunch and "bird nest" cupcakes (p. 71) for dessert. (These cupcakes could be made by the Young Women in one of the classes.)

"SUPER SATURDAY IN SPRING"
Program Outline and Assignment Sheet

_____Opening song: "On a Golden Springtime," *Children's Songbook*, p. 88

_____Opening prayer

_____Welcome: Include the objective of the program

_____Classes: Each young woman will attend the classes she signed up for.
        (Plan for classes to end at lunch time.)

_____Blessing on the food

_____Lunch: Each girl should bring a sack lunch. Provide punch.

_____Speaker: Be sure to include these points:
        *The knowledge we learn in this life will stay with us always.
        *We need to increase our knowledge in all areas: the gospel, education, hobbies, etc.
        *Learning how to do new things can increase our self-worth.

_____Classes: Each young woman will attend the classes she signed up for.
        (Plan for the classes to end in time to have a 15-minute closing.)

_____Closing: Have the "bird nest" cupcakes for dessert, see p. 71.
        This is a great time for the girls to show off the items they made.

_____Closing song: "There Is Sunshine in My Soul Today," hymnbook, p. 227

_____Closing prayer

More Assignments to Consider

_____Preparation of invitations   _____Decorations organizer
_____Preparation of programs   _____Setup organizer
_____Classes organizer   _____Cleanup organizer
_____Drink/dessert organizer

INSTRUCTIONS FOR MAKING THE INVITATIONS AND PROGRAMS

INVITATIONS: Make a copy of the invitations (p. 72). Write or type your information on them. Copy them onto pastel-colored paper. Cut them apart (there are two on each page). Optional: Glue a thin layer of moss at the base of the flower stems and a raffia bow at the center of the flower pot among the moss. Distribute one to each young woman one week prior to the event.

PROGRAMS: Make a copy of the program border (p. 74). Write or type your program information inside the border. Copy the program front (p. 73) onto pastel-colored paper with the border on the reverse side of the paper. Fold in half.

INFORMATION ABOUT THE CLASSES:

*You will want to schedule several classes at the same time. This will give the young women a chance to choose which classes they want to take. You may also want to schedule the same class more than once to provide more opportunities for each young woman to attend the classes she desires.

*Be sure to plan classes that are low in cost and easy enough for the young women to do. You want to be sure each young woman finishes the day feeling good about her abilities and talents.

*Be sure to plan the appropriate amount of time for each class. You want each young woman to go home with a few finished items and a sense of accomplishment.

*You may want to include ideas from the young women when planning classes. After all, they know what they like.

IDEAS FOR CLASSES

BOTTLED OILS and BATH SALTS

You can usually find small decorative bottles with corks at craft or dollar stores for a reasonable price. Select several varied shapes and sizes. *For the oils:* Drop small dried flowers and leaves into the bottom of a bottle. Use a small funnel to fill the bottle with baby oil and place the cork in it. *For the bath salts:* Use a small funnel to fill the bottle with bath salts and place the cork in it. *To seal the bottles:* Melt paraffin wax in a double boiler. Dip the bottle neck into the wax covering to just below the cork to seal it. Let the wax harden. (You will need to repeat the dipping process several times.) *To decorate the bottles:* Use raffia to tie bows around the neck of each sealed bottle. Glue small dried flowers and leaves at the bow center.

DECOUPAGED TERRA COTTA POTS:

You can buy small terra cotta clay pots at craft stores and use paper napkins to cover them. (An overall floral printed napkin gives the best appearance.) *For each project:* Cut a napkin into small pieces. Add water to white glue to thin. Use a small paintbrush to apply glue to a small area on the outside of the pot. Place a napkin piece onto the glued area. Brush more glue over the piece to saturate it and make it adhere it to the pot. Repeat this process, overlapping the pieces to cover the pot outside (overlap the top edge to the pot inside and the bottom edge to the underneath side). Repeat this process to cover the pot inside; let dry. Spray with an acrylic sealer.

BIRD NEST CUPCAKES:
Bake any flavor of cupcakes according to the package directions. Frost each one with chocolate frosting. Place some shredded coconut in a plastic bag, add one drop of green food coloring and shake to mix the color into the coconut. If necessary, repeat with one drop of food coloring at a time until the coconut is a light green (to imitate the color of grass). *For each cupcake:* Sprinkle some coconut onto the frosting and place three pastel-speckled jelly beans in the center for "bird eggs."

DECORATIVE BOOKS:
Usually you can find old hardback books at thrift stores for next to nothing. Choose ones with desirable sizes and colors. *For each project:* You will need two books, one slightly larger than the other. Stack the smaller one on top of the larger one. Use raffia to wrap them as you would wrap ribbon around a present. Use raffia to tie a large bow and glue it at the center of the top book. Glue dried or silk flowers and leaves at the bow's center.

BROWN PAPER HEARTS:
For each project: Cut a heart (approximately 6.5"x6") from a brown paper grocery sack or brown craft paper. Cut a heart slightly smaller than the paper heart from desired fabric (using pinking shears to cut the fabric makes a nice effect). Add water to white glue to thin. Use a small brush to apply the glue to the back of the fabric heart, place it centered onto the paper heart; let dry. Cut a square of brown paper slightly larger than the paper heart. Apply a thin layer of full-strength glue to the backside of the paper heart along the edges (be sure to leave an unglued area for stuffing the heart). Place onto the paper square; let dry. Stuff the heart with a small amount of polyester fiberfill (just until it is slightly puffy). Glue the opening closed; let dry. Trim the paper square even with the heart. Glue ribbon for a hanger. Use ribbon to tie two bows and glue one to each side of the heart at the upper corners. Cut various sized rectangles of assorted fabric scraps and glue them to the heart. Glue buttons, beads, charms, etc., on the fabric scraps.

PONYTAIL HOLDERS: *For each project:* Cut a 5"x45" strip of desired fabric. With right sides together, fold the fabric strip in half lengthwise. Sew along the long edge using a 1/2" seam allowance; turn. Iron each end under 1/2". Cut an 11" length of 1/4" wide elastic. Use a safety pin to guide the elastic through the fabric tube; overlap the elastic ends and sew. Handstitch the opening closed.

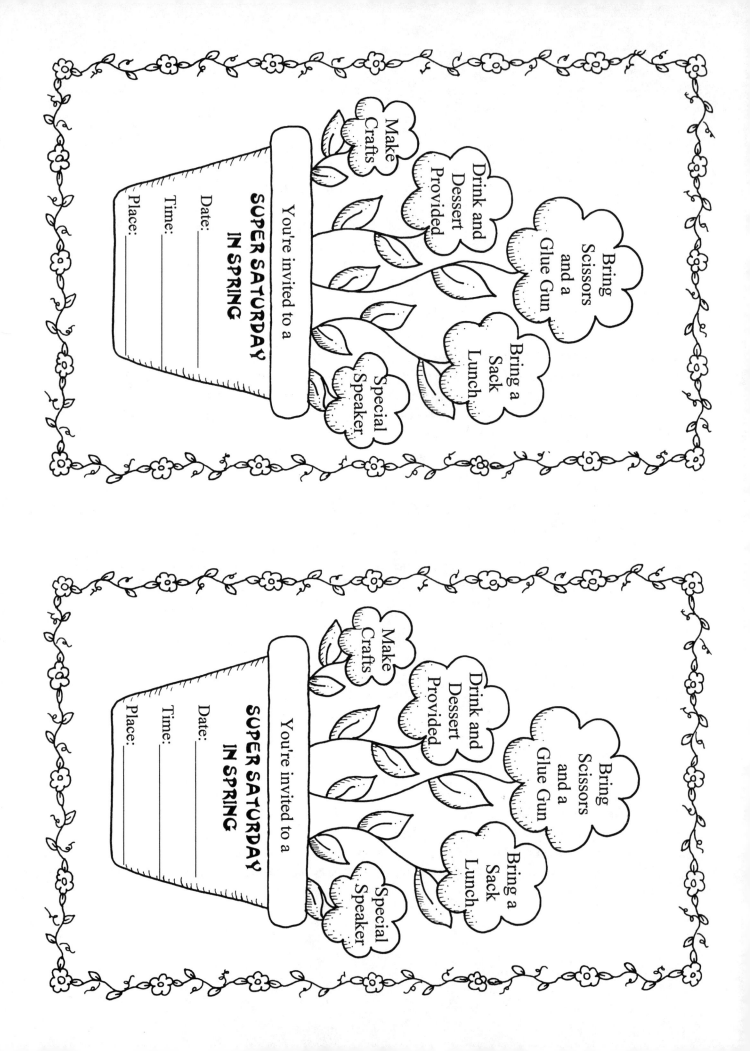

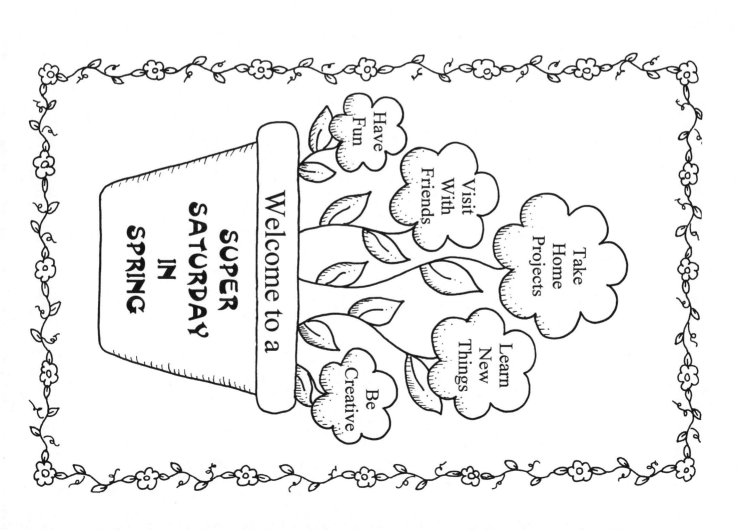

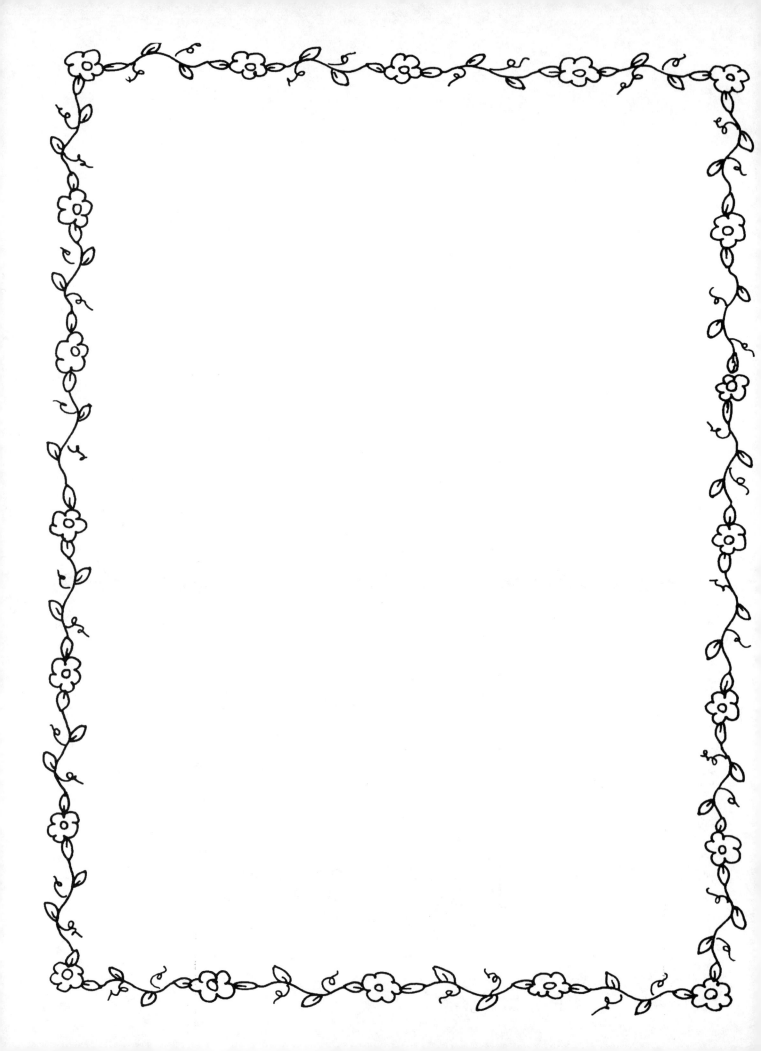

"FASHIONABLE FUN"

"...that women adorn themselves in modest apparel..." 1 Timothy 2:9

OBJECTIVE:

To prepare each young woman to make wise fashion choices and to provide a fun afternoon for her to spend with her mother.

MATERIALS NEEDED:

An invitation for each young woman to be invited, see pp. 81-82
A program for everyone to be invited, see pp. 83-84
A handout for everyone to be invited, see p. 82
A copy of the "Fashionable Fun" skit for the director and each participant, pp. 77-80
A spotlight, props and costumes for the skit.

PREPARATION:

1. Make the assignments using the suggested Program Outline/Assignment Sheet, p. 76.
2. Assign the parts for the skit.
3. Schedule practice times for the skit, including a dress rehearsal.
4. Assign the speaker.
5. Schedule the church building for the afternoon of the event, allowing for setup time that morning or the evening before.

SUGGESTIONS FOR DECORATIONS:

1. Stack fashion magazines at each table for a centerpiece, or cut the fashion pages from magazines or department store catalogs into puzzle-shaped pieces and scatter at the table center.
2. Copy the border from p. 84 onto orange paper and use as place mats for the table settings.
3. Hang fashion pages from magazines or department store catalogs on the walls along with giant question marks.
4. Set the tables up leaving a center aisle to create a runway for the models in the skit to use. You may even want to run crepe paper between the tables to emphasize the runway.

SUGGESTIONS FOR LUNCHEON MENU:

Make it a light luncheon. Chicken salad sandwiches, vegetable soup, water, or soda pop to drink, ice cream and sugar cookies for dessert.

"FASHIONABLE FUN"
Program Outline and Assignment Sheet

_____Opening song: "Choose the Right," hymnbook, p. 239

_____Opening prayer and blessing on the food

_____Welcome: Include the objective of the program.

_____Luncheon: A light luncheon:
> Chicken salad sandwiches, vegetable soup, water or soda pop to drink, ice cream and sugar cookies for dessert.

_____Presentation of the "Fashionable Fun" skit

_____Speaker: Be sure to include these points:
> *Do I feel comfortable in my clothes?
> *What image do I want to send?
> *How would I feel about my outfit if Christ visited me today?

_____Closing remarks: Distribute the "Puzzled Heart" handouts.

_____Closing song: "Teach Me to Walk in the Light," hymnbook, p. 304

_____Closing prayer

More Assignments to Consider

_____Preparation of invitations   _____Luncheon organizer
_____Preparation of programs   _____Decorations organizer
_____Preparation of handouts   _____Setup organizer
_____Skit director/organizer   _____Cleanup organizer

INSTRUCTIONS FOR MAKING THE INVITATIONS, PROGRAMS AND HANDOUTS

INVITATIONS: Make a copy of the invitation front (p. 81). Write or type your information on the invitation. Copy this onto orange paper with the puzzle (p. 82) on the reverse side of the paper. Cut the invitation into the puzzle pieces and place in an envelope. Distribute one to each young woman one week prior to the event.

PROGRAMS: Make a copy of the program border (p. 84). Write or type your program information inside the border. Copy the program front (p. 83) onto orange paper with the border on the reverse side of the paper. Fold in half.

HANDOUTS: _Puzzled Hearts:_ Glue puzzle pieces (from old puzzles) onto a small purchased wood heart overlapping them to cover the heart. Paint it ivory. Glue ivory ribbon for a hanger. Glue a ribbon bow at the center top of the heart. Glue small buttons, beads, etc. at the bow center. When distributing the handouts, suggest young women need not have a "puzzled heart" when it comes to fashion if they "adorn themselves in modest apparel" _(1 Timothy 2:9)._

76

"FASHIONABLE FUN"
Fashion Show Skit

PLAYERS:

Freda Choose - a 12-year-old young woman

Mom - a woman of appropriate age to have a 12-year-old daughter

Narrator - a young woman's leader or an older young woman

Models - Izzy Looking, Mora Money, Ineeta Iron, Maude Est, Missy Matched, Lotta Makeup, Lotta Jewelry, Shirley BeReady, Terri Cloth, Sharon Everything, Seena TooMuch, Carra TooLittle and Wanda Change - a young woman for each model (she should dress according to her part in the script)

SETTING:

A fashion show with a runway for the models and a podium for the narrator. Start with the lights out and a spotlight on Freda Choose and her mom.

FREDA CHOOSE: *(narrating to the audience)*

Hi. My name is Freda Choose. I've just turned 12 and am entering Young Women this Sunday. I wanted a new dress for the occasion. So I asked my mom if she would pick one out for me. Her response surprised me!

MOM:

Honey, you're growing up. You're a young woman now. You're Freda Choose. It's time for you to start making some of your own fashion decisions. You need to choose a style that fits your personality and that you feel comfortable with. Just remember that there are many things to think about in style and fashion.

FREDA CHOOSE:

But, Mom, I don't know what my style is or what it should be. Oh, now I'm really puzzled!

FREDA CHOOSE: *(narrating to the audience)*

There I was, puzzled and confused. What did she mean, "There are many things to think about in style and fashion?" I started thinking about what my style might be when I remembered a fashion show I saw on TV last week.

Turn off the spotlight and turn on the lights to begin the fashion show.

NARRATOR:

Have you ever noticed how many different styles there are these days? I know it can be puzzling with all the choices to be made in fashion wear. Luckily we have some delightful models with us today who will be helping us to make our fashion choices. So, I'd like to invite all of you to just sit back and enjoy our show.

Model #1 — "Izzy Looking" enters the runway.

NARRATOR:

Here is our first model. Her name is Izzy Looking. Izzy is wearing an attractive and modest skirt and blouse. Izzy, like the rest of us, enjoys a glance now and then from the boys. She has discovered that the shorter her skirt gets *(Izzy uses her hands to slightly raise her skirt while acting as if a boy is noticing her)*, the more "he" looks. This seems harmless to Izzy, but she doesn't realize what message she is sending to the boys. Will they respect her or just think she is eager to please them? Maybe Izzy should worry less if "he" is looking and more about her image. Thank you, Izzy. *(Izzy leaves the runway.)*

Model #2 — "Mora Money" enters the runway.

NARRATOR:

Wow, would you look at our next model, Mora Money? Isn't her outfit gorgeous with the matching accessories and all? Mora paid a fortune for this outfit! *(Mora pulls some play money out from her purse and waves it around.)* There's nothing wrong in spending a little extra every now and then, within your budget, of course. But Mora believes that the more money she pays, the better her outfit is. She never buys on sale. What's going to happen when Mora has to live on a tight budget? Will she be able to control her spending or will she go into debt? Thank you, Mora. *(Mora leaves the runway.)*

Model #3 — "Ineeta Iron" enters the runway.

NARRATOR:

This model, Ineeta Iron, is wearing a lovely pantsuit. Ineeta is one of our busiest models. She doesn't have much free time and therefore doesn't like to do things she feels are unnecessary. Unfortunately, she doesn't believe ironing is necessary. *(Ineeta makes a face at the thought of ironing.)* She's a beautiful girl, but just think how much nicer she would look if her outfit was nicely pressed. Thank you, Ineeta. *(Ineeta leaves the runway.)*

Model #4 — "Maude Est" enters the runway.

NARRATOR:

The name of this model is Maude Est. She is wearing an attractive jumper with a shirt underneath. Notice her jumper is below or at her knee and the neckline is very modest. *(Maude points to her hem and neckline.)* Maude could and does wear this to church. When choosing her clothes, she asks herself, "What if I saw Christ today? Would he approve of my outfit?" Thank you, Maude. *(Maude leaves the runway.)*

Model #5 — "Missy Matched" enters the runway.

NARRATOR:

Our next model often has a very interesting look. As you can see, Missy Matched is sporting clothes that just do not quite go together. Notice her left sock is different from her right sock. *(Missy raises her pants to show her socks.)* Missy often finds herself at school like this. She doesn't necessarily enjoy it, but she's in such a hurry in the mornings. She jumps out of bed and just throws on whatever she can find. Missy says she's just too tired to get up early enough to match her clothing or to do it the night before. Thank you, Missy. *(Missy leaves the runway.)*

Models #6 & #7 — "Lotta Makeup" and "Lotta Jewelry" enter the runway together.

NARRATOR:
Here we have the Lotta sisters. Lotta Makeup and Lotta Jewelry. They believe that if a little is good, a lot is even better. Lotta Makeup spends two hours every morning to achieve her look. *(Lotta Makeup pulls lipstick from her pocket or purse and acts as if she's applying it to her lips.)* Lotta Jewelry has more necklaces and earrings than the accessory store at the mall! *(Lotta Jewelry points to her necklaces, earrings, etc.)* The Lotta sisters pride themselves on their looks. I wonder if they've ever heard the expression, "Less is more"? Thank you, Lotta Makeup and Lotta Jewelry. *(The Lotta sisters leave the runway.)*

Model #8 — "Shirley BeReady" enters the runway.

NARRATOR:
Our next model, Shirley BeReady, always looks very nice and neat. Notice her clothes are very clean and well pressed. She takes the time to prepare her wardrobe the night before. *(Shirley points to her watch.)* She believes that being prepared and looking neat will help her to achieve success in her life. Thank you, Shirley. *(Shirley leaves the runway.)*

Model #9 — "Terri Cloth" enters the runway.

NARRATOR:
As you can see, our next model, Terri Cloth, is into comfort. She feels very comfortable in her robe. Of course you should feel comfortable in your clothes, but Terri *only* wears her robe. She even wants to wear it to school! *(Terri holds up a notebook and pencil.)* Maybe Terri needs to understand the compromise between comfort and the appropriate clothing for the appropriate activity. *(Terri gives a puzzled look.)* Thank you, Terri. *(Terri leaves the runway.)*

Model #10 — "Sharon Everything" enters the runway.

NARRATOR:
Isn't she lovely? Her name is Sharon Everything. Sharon believes in sharing clothes with her friends. However, she doesn't like to spend money on her own clothes, so the sharing seems to go only one way. *(Sharon puts her hand out to a friend alongside the runway. The friend hands her an outfit on a hanger and Sharon holds it up as if to see what it would look like on her.)* Her friends didn't mind at first, but now they are getting tired of it. Besides, Sharon hasn't created her own style; she is just imitating her friends' styles. Thank you, Sharon. *(Sharon leaves the runway.)*

Model #11 — "Seena TooMuch" enters the runway.

NARRATOR:
This model is Seena TooMuch. She's seen just about everything when it comes to fashion. She's seen short skirts, green hair, nose rings and many other extremes. *(Seena points to her skirt, hair, nose, etc., and shakes her head in disapproval.)* She decided that she likes to be modest in her clothing and stay away from the extreme styles. Her outfit today is a good example of what Seena likes. She feels comfortable with herself and doesn't feel like she needs to draw attention to herself with extreme fashion styles. Thank you, Seena. *(Seena leaves the runway.)*

Model #12 — "Carra TooLittle" enters the runway.

NARRATOR:
Carra TooLittle is the name of this model. She is wearing her favorite outfit. She obviously wears it often. It seems to be full of holes and is a little dirty looking. *(Carra tries to brush off the dirt with her hand and then acts as if it's no big deal anyway.)* Carra is aware of the condition of her outfit but just doesn't seem to care. She likes it and is going to wear it anyway. She figures what you look like on the outside doesn't matter; it's what's on the inside that matters. Of course, it is what's on the inside that matters, but cleanliness on the outside should not be overlooked. Thank you, Carra. *(Carra leaves the runway.)*

Model #13 — "Wanda Change" enters the runway.

NARRATOR:
Our last model today is Wanda Change. Wanda attended a fashion show similar to this one a few months ago. She realized she had some of the same fashion attitudes as some of the models. She felt she wasn't always making the right fashion choices *(Wanda lowers her head and shakes it to say, "No.")* and wanted to change to be more like Maude Est, Shirley BeReady and Seena TooMuch. *(Wanda raises her head and nods it to say, "Yes.")* Today she is wearing an outfit that she feels is very comfortable, modest, clean and neat. She plans to be successful in whatever career she pursues and knows that her Heavenly Father would be pleased with her fashion choices. Thank you, Wanda. *(Wanda leaves the runway.)*

NARRATOR:
Didn't the models today do a great job! Let's applaud them for all their hard work. *(Pause for a moment of applause.)* I hope each of us can learn from these models today as we try to develop our own fashion attitudes and styles.

Lights go off and spotlight returns on Freda.

FREDA: *(narrating to the audience)*
That was quite a fashion show. But it does help me to put the pieces of this fashion puzzle together. Well, I gotta go now. I'm off to the mall to buy that new dress.

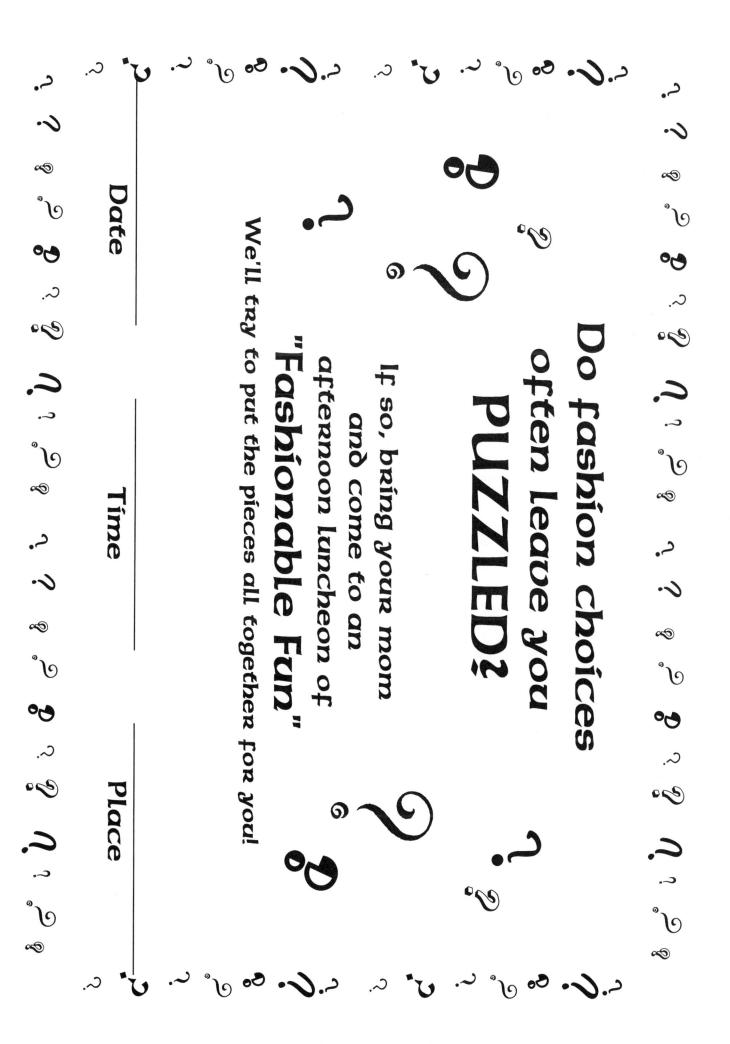

Do fashion choices often leave you PUZZLED?

If so, bring your mom and come to an afternoon luncheon of

"Fashionable Fun"

We'll try to put the pieces all together for you!

Date

Time

Place

Welcome to
an afternoon of
"FASHIONABLE FUN"

We hope to
help you
take some
of the
question marks
out of fashion!

"BUILD THE KINGDOM THROUGH RIGHTEOUS SERVICE"

"...that ye may learn that when ye are in the service of your fellow beings
ye are in the service of your God." *Mosiah 2:17*

OBJECTIVE:

To encourage each young woman to perform acts of service for others. Also to provide an opportunity for her to spend a fun morning with her father as she increases her knowledge and skills in working with tools. (She will make a birdhouse that she can give to someone she feels needs some special attention.)

MATERIALS NEEDED:

An invitation for each young woman to be invited, see p. 87
A program for everyone to be invited, see pp. 91-92
A handout for everyone to be invited, see p. 93
A birdhouse kit for each young woman to be invited, see p. 89
Plenty of hammers and nails for the young women to use to assemble their birdhouse kits
The tools mentioned in the "Tools" handout, see p. 93 (to be used by the speaker)

PREPARATION:

1. Make the assignments using the suggested Program Outline/Assignment Sheet, p. 86.
2. Assign the speaker.
3. Arrange for someone to cut out the wood pieces for the birdhouse kits.
4. Schedule the church building for the morning of the event, allowing enough time the evening before to set up and decorate.

SUGGESTIONS FOR DECORATIONS:

1. Use clean drop cloths or black plastic for tablecloths. (Try to make it look like a workshop.)
2. Copy the "Tools" handout from p. 93 onto yellow paper to use as place mats for the table settings.
3. Set tools and wood pieces on the tables for centerpieces.

SUGGESTIONS FOR BREAKFAST:

Ham, eggs, muffins, fresh fruit, juice and milk to drink. (Remember, the invitations promise most of these items!)

"BUILD THE KINGDOM THROUGH RIGHTEOUS SERVICE"
Program Outline and Assignment Sheet

_____Opening song: "Have I Done Any Good?" hymnbook, p. 223

_____Opening prayer and blessing on the food

_____Welcome: Include the objective of the program.

_____Breakfast: Ham, eggs, muffins, fresh fruit, juice and milk to drink

_____Speaker: Be sure to include the tools and the ideas covered from the
                 "Tools" handout, see p. 93.

_____Building of the birdhouses, see p. 88.
                 (Each young woman will assemble one with the help of her father.)

_____Sharing of testimonies: Allow time for anyone who wishes to share their
                 feelings about service.

_____Closing Remarks: Distribute the "Tools" and/or "Wood" handouts.

_____Closing song: "Because I Have Been Given Much," hymnbook, p. 219

_____Closing prayer

More Assignments to Consider

_____Preparation of invitations   _____Breakfast organizer
_____Preparation of programs   _____Decorations organizer
_____Preparation of handouts   _____Setup organizer
_____Birdhouse kits organizer   _____Cleanup organizer

INSTRUCTIONS FOR MAKING THE INVITATIONS, PROGRAMS AND HANDOUTS

INVITATIONS: Make a copy of the "inside message" (p. 87). Write or type your information on the invitation. Copy it and the "outside message" onto yellow paper. Cut each one out along the outside border. Fold the "outside message" into half and glue the side edges together, leaving it open at the top to create an envelope. Fold the "inside message" in half and glue it closed. Let each dry. Insert the "inside message" into the "outside message" envelope. Distribute one to each young woman one week prior to the event.

PROGRAMS: Make a copy of the program border (p. 92). Write or type your program information inside the border. Copy the program front (p. 91) onto yellow paper with the border on the reverse side of the paper, making sure the tools are right side up at the bottom of the border when folded. Fold in half.

HANDOUTS: Supplied are two handout ideas. _Tools:_ Copy the "Tools" handout (p. 93) onto yellow paper. _Wood:_ Copy the "Wood" handouts (p. 90) onto yellow paper. Cut each one out along the outside border. Thumb tack or nail one to a piece of wood. (Optional: Write the message directly onto a piece of wood with a permanent marker.)

Inside Message

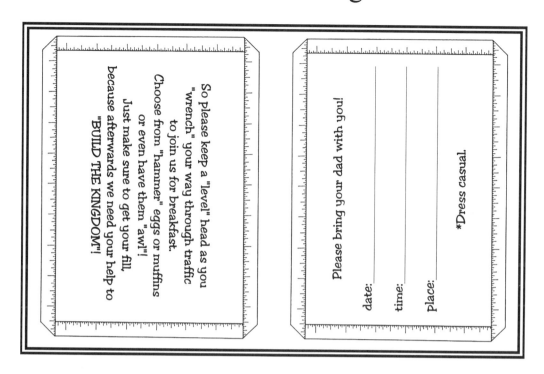

So please keep a "level" head as you
"wrench" your way through traffic
to join us for breakfast.
Choose from "hammer" eggs or muffins
or even have them "awl"!
Just make sure to get your fill,
because afterwards we need your help to
"BUILD THE KINGDOM"!

Please bring your dad with you!

date:

time:

place:

*Dress casual.

Outside Message

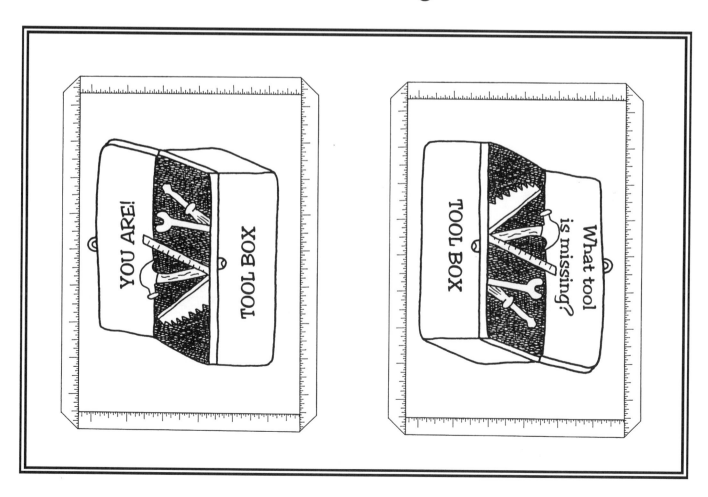

YOU ARE!

TOOL BOX

TOOL BOX

What tool
is missing?

FOR EACH BIRDHOUSE KIT:

1. Use the patterns on p. 89 to cut out each wood piece.

2. Use a 1 1/2" drill bit to drill the hole in the front piece.

3. Nail the back piece with it sitting flush on the back of the base piece.

4. Nail one side piece with it sitting flush on each side of the base piece and flush against the back piece.

5. Nail the front piece with it sitting flush against the side pieces. The base piece will extend 1 1/4" forward from the front piece.

6. Nail the smaller roof piece so that the back of it is flush with the back of the birdhouse and even with the roof angle. The roof piece will extend 1 1/2" forward from the front piece.

7. Nail the other roof piece so that the back of it is flush with the back of the birdhouse and extends over the first roof piece. The roof piece will extend 1 1/2" forward from the front piece.

8. Paint or stain the birdhouse; let dry.

9. Tape the included poem to the birdhouse (see p. 90).

"BUILD THE KINGDOM THROUGH RIGHTEOUS SERVICE"

Birdhouse Pattern

*All pieces are cut from 3/4" pine. (See p. 88 to assemble the birdhouse.)

1. Cut two pieces using the front/back pattern shown. You will drill a 1 1/2" hole in the front piece only.
2. Cut one of each roof piece using the dimensions shown.
3. Cut one base piece using the dimensions shown.
4. Cut two side pieces, each 4 1/2" x 3 1/2" x 3/4".

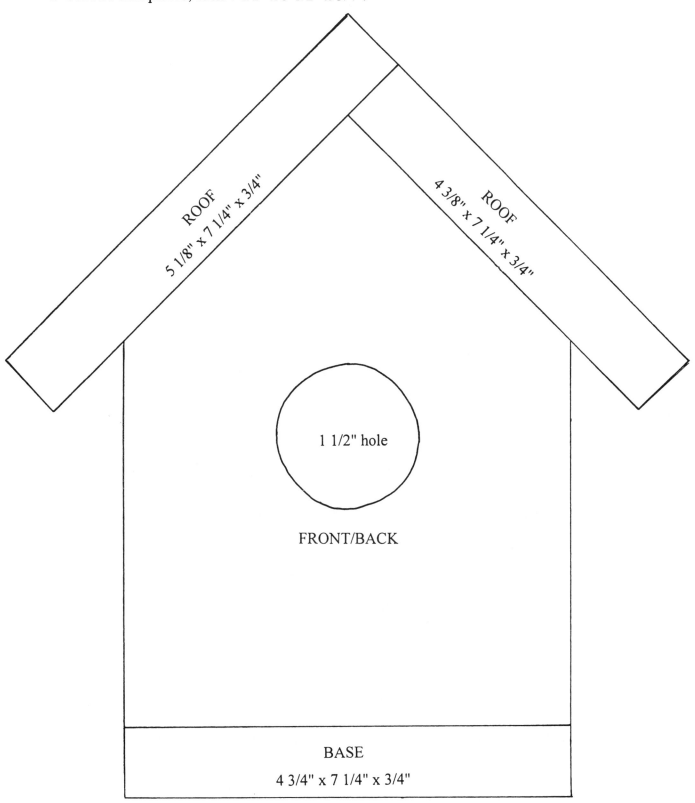

ROOF
5 1/8" x 7 1/4" x 3/4"

ROOF
4 3/8" x 7 1/4" x 3/4"

1 1/2" hole

FRONT/BACK

BASE
4 3/4" x 7 1/4" x 3/4"

Copy onto yellow paper.
Cut each poem out along the outside border.

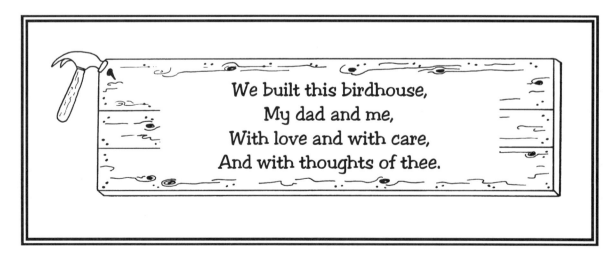

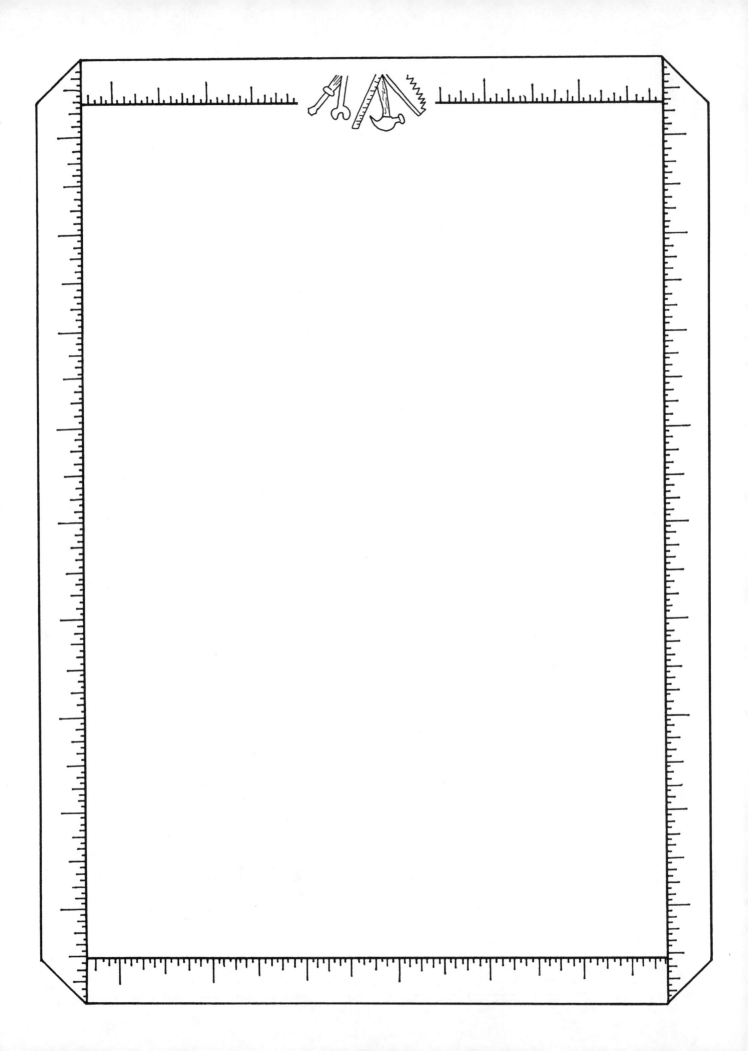

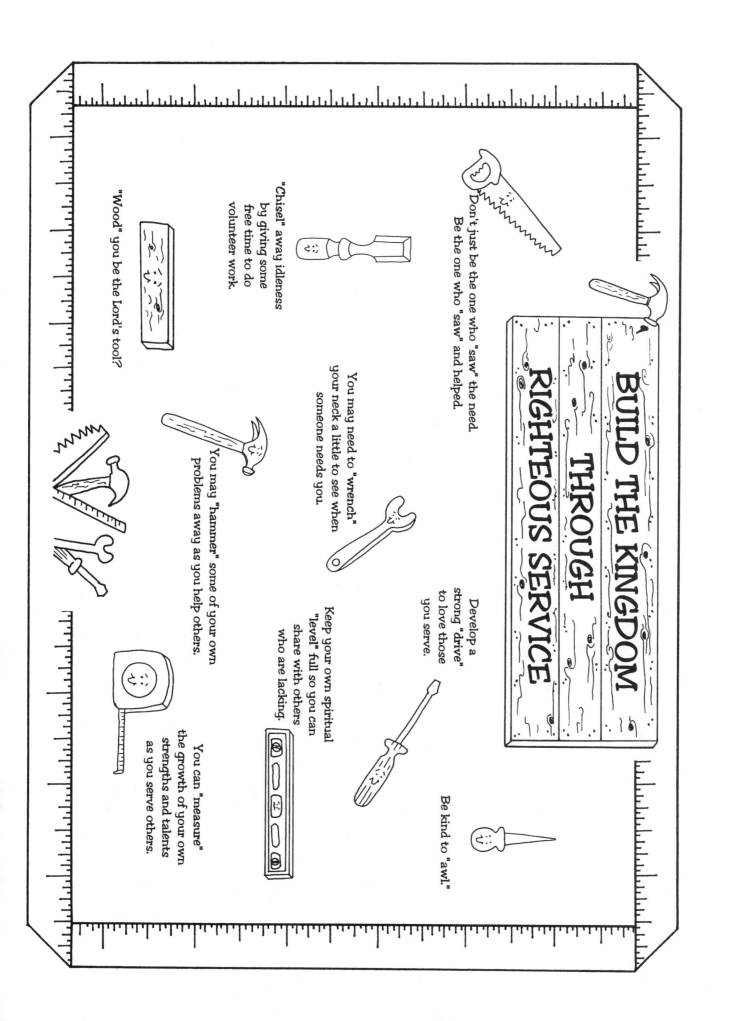

BUILD THE KINGDOM THROUGH RIGHTEOUS SERVICE

Don't just be the one who "saw" the need.
Be the one who "saw" and helped.

"Chisel" away idleness by giving some free time to do volunteer work.

"Wood" you be the Lord's tool?

You may need to "wrench" your neck a little to see when someone needs you.

You may "hammer" some of your own problems away as you help others.

Keep your own spiritual "level" full so you can share with others who are lacking.

Develop a strong "drive" to love those you serve.

You can "measure" the growth of your own strengths and talents as you serve others.

Be kind to "awl."

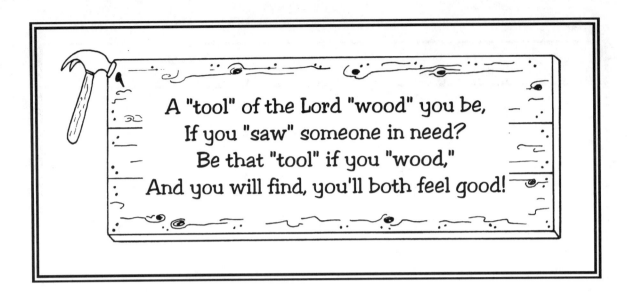

A "tool" of the Lord "wood" you be,
If you "saw" someone in need?
Be that "tool" if you "wood,"
And you will find, you'll both feel good!

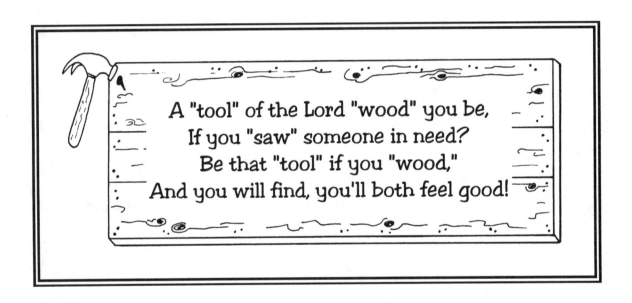

A "tool" of the Lord "wood" you be,
If you "saw" someone in need?
Be that "tool" if you "wood,"
And you will find, you'll both feel good!

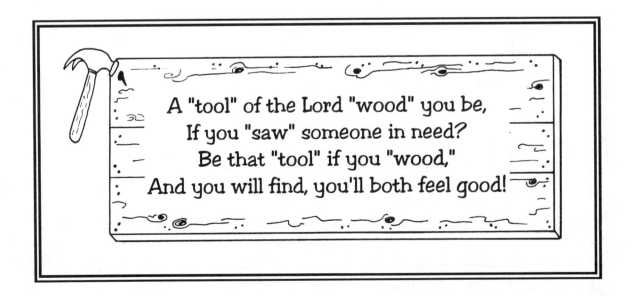

A "tool" of the Lord "wood" you be,
If you "saw" someone in need?
Be that "tool" if you "wood,"
And you will find, you'll both feel good!

"WHAT MAKES A HERO?"

"The integrity of the upright shall guide them..." *Proverbs 11:3*

OBJECTIVE:

To encourage each young woman to choose heroes who have integrity and to provide an opportunity for her to share with others who her heroes are and why. Also to help her realize that she can have the attributes of a hero.

MATERIALS NEEDED:

An invitation for everyone to be invited, see p. 98

A program for everyone to be invited, see pp. 99-100

A handout for everyone to be invited, see pp. 101-106

A podium or microphone for the young women to use when sharing their heroes (optional)

PREPARATION:

1. Make the assignments using the suggested Program Outline/Assignment Sheet, p. 96.
2. Assign the speaker (she will make a real hero sandwich as she talks; see the "How to Make a Hero" talk presentation, p. 97).
3. Assign some of the young women (or all of them) to be prepared to share who their heroes are and why they admire them.
4. Schedule enough time to set up and decorate the afternoon of the event.

SUGGESTIONS FOR DECORATIONS:

1. Copy the program front from p. 99 onto purple cardstock paper. Fold in half. Set one on each table for a centerpiece.
2. Copy the border from p. 100 onto purple paper to use as place mats for the table settings.
3. Obtain large pictures of scriptural heroes or Church leaders from your ward library to hang on the walls (i.e., Nephi, Esther, Joseph Smith, President Hinkley, or one of the prophets' wives, etc.).

SUGGESTIONS FOR DINNER MENU:

Hero sandwiches (make sure to include all the ingredients mentioned in the talk, see p. 97) and chips for dinner, water or punch to drink and cookies for dessert. (Try to keep it simple.)

"WHAT MAKES A HERO?"
Program Outline and Assignment Sheet

_____Opening song: "True to the Faith," hymnbook, p. 254

_____Opening prayer and blessing on the food

_____Welcome: Include the objective of the program.

_____Speaker: See the "How to Make a Hero" talk presentation, p. 97.

_____Dinner: Have each young woman make her own hero sandwich.
Hero sandwiches and chips for dinner, water or punch to drink and cookies for dessert. (Keep it simple.)

_____Sharing of heroes by the young women

_____Closing remarks: Distribute the "How to Make a Hero" handouts.

_____Closing song: "Stand for the Right," _Children's Songbook_, p. 159

_____Closing prayer

More Assignments to Consider

_____Preparation of invitations   _____Decorations organizer
_____Preparation of programs   _____Setup organizer
_____Preparation of handouts   _____Cleanup organizer
_____Dinner organizer

INSTRUCTIONS FOR MAKING THE INVITATIONS, PROGRAMS AND HANDOUTS

INVITATIONS: Make a copy of the invitation (p. 98). Write or type your information on it. Copy this onto purple paper. Fold in half and then in half again with the sandwich on the front and the information on the inside. Distribute one to everyone invited one week prior to the event.

PROGRAMS: Make a copy of the program border (p. 100). Write or type your program information inside the border. Copy the program front (p. 99) onto purple paper with the border on the reverse side of the paper. Fold in half.

HANDOUTS: _"How to Make a Hero" Sandwiches:_ See pp. 101-106. Copy the "bread" pieces onto ivory paper. Copy the "spread" pieces onto white paper. Copy the "meat" pieces onto tan paper. Copy the "cheese" pieces onto light orange paper. Copy the "lettuce" pieces onto light green paper. Cut out each piece. _For each handout:_ Stack one of each item to form the sandwich in this order; bottom bread, spread, meat, cheese, lettuce and the top bread on top. Use a hole punch to make a hole where indicated through all layers. Insert a brass paper fastener to secure the sandwich together.

"HOW TO MAKE A HERO"
Talk Presentation

The following is an outline for the talk and goes along with the handouts. You may want to elaborate on each item as you present your talk.

1. **WHAT MAKES A HERO?**

   I am going to make a hero sandwich. While I do, I will be relating ways we can make ourselves into heroes. By following these suggestions, we can each gain personal integrity and develop the qualities of a hero.

2. **HOLD UP THE BOTTOM PIECE OF BREAD:**

   This piece of bread is the foundation for the hero sandwich. We need to "start with the right foundation," which is the gospel of Jesus Christ.

3. **SPREAD SOME MAYONNAISE ONTO THE BREAD:**

   The sandwich would be quite dry without some mayonnaise spread onto it. We need to enrich others' lives as we "spread the gospel."

4. **PLACE SOME MEAT ONTO THE BREAD:**

   The meat is important to the sandwich; it provides a good filling for it. We need to "attend our church 'meat'ings" so we can be filled spiritually.

5. **PLACE SOME CHEESE ONTO THE BREAD:**

   There are many kinds of cheeses to choose from when making a hero sandwich. One thing that we need to remember is to always "'cheese' the right" in all our thoughts and actions.

6. **PLACE SOME LETTUCE AND OTHER GARNISHES ONTO THE BREAD:**

   Garnishes, such as lettuce, tomato, onion and pickles, add flavor and make the sandwich colorful and more appealing. "'Lettuce' garnish our own and others' lives with spiritual qualities" like charity, patience, service, etc.

7. **PLACE THE TOP PIECE OF BREAD ONTO THE SANDWICH:**

   We've made a hero sandwich. We've also learned some ways to help us gain hero qualities. There are many more things we need to do also, such as prayer, scripture study, etc. By doing these types of things, the Spirit will be with us. Real heroes have the Spirit with them. Now I would like to tell you about one of my favorite heroes. (Talk briefly about one of your favorite scriptural heroes or Church leaders or their wives.)

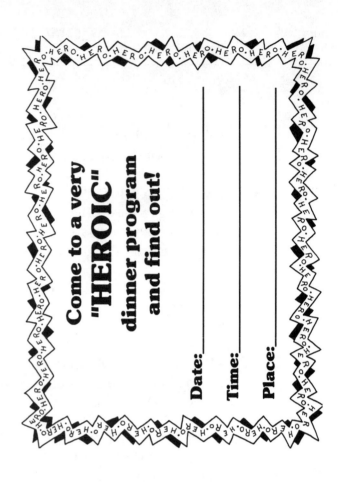

Come to a very "HEROIC" dinner program and find out!

Date: _____

Time: _____

Place: _____

How do you make a HERO?

What makes a
HERO?

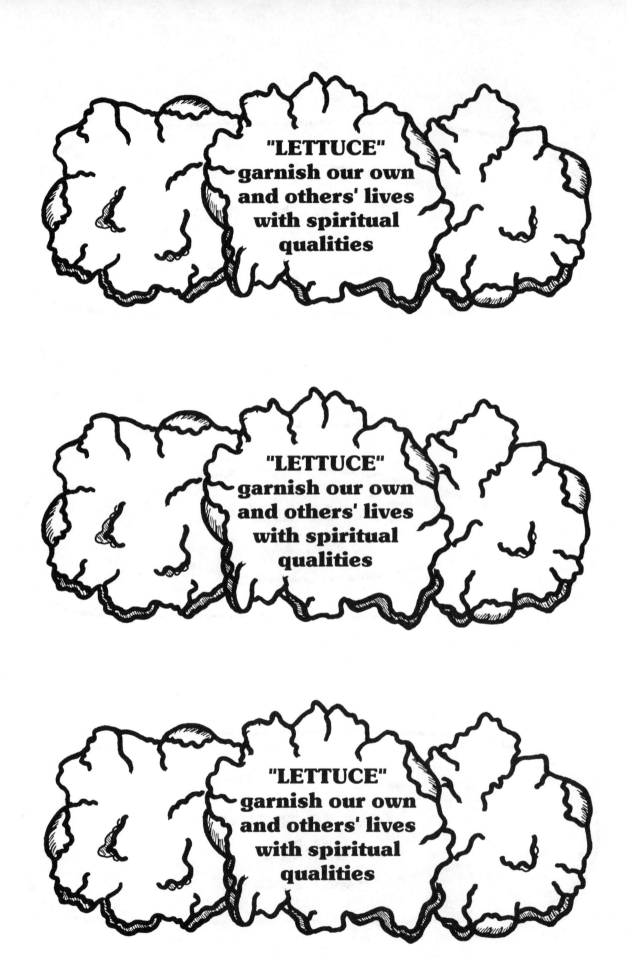

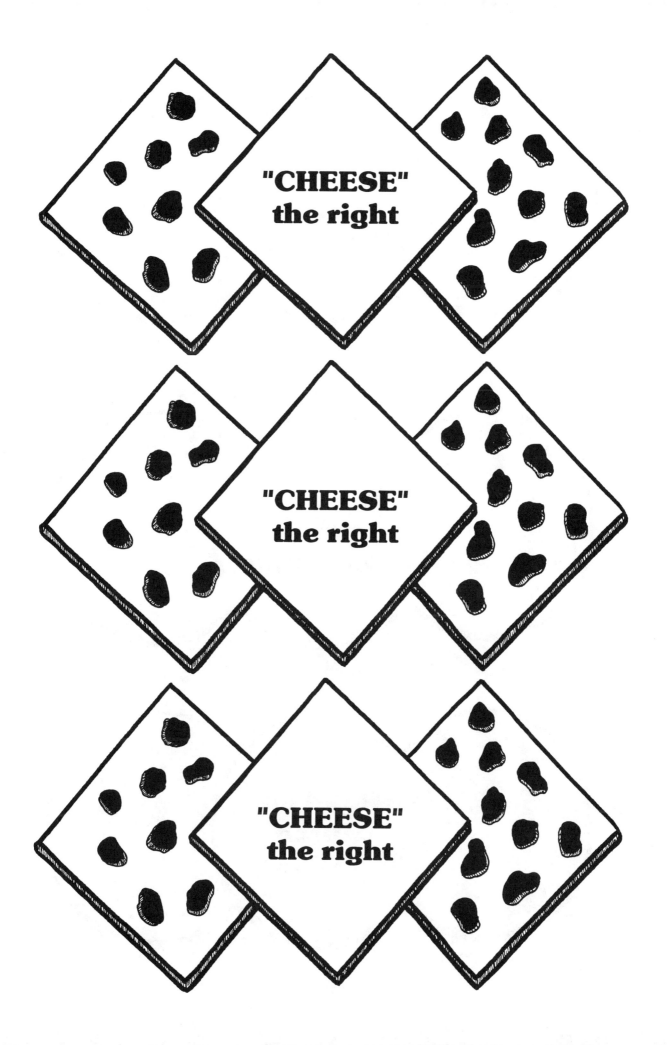

**Start with
the right
"FOUNDATION"**

**Start with
the right
"FOUNDATION"**

**Start with
the right
"FOUNDATION"**

"Celebrate a VALUE-able Harvest"

"...all men shall reap a reward of their works, according to that which they have been..."
Alma 9:28

OBJECTIVE:

To reinforce the Young Women values for each young woman and to provide an opportunity for her to share her personal progress achievements with her parents.

MATERIALS NEEDED:

An invitation for each young woman to be invited, see p. 120

A program for everyone to be invited, see pp. 121-122

The "VALUE-able Harvest" garland pieces for each young woman, see pp. 133-140

A copy of "The VALUE-able Harvest" skit for the director and each participant,
  pp. 111-119

Props and costumes for the skit

PREPARATION:

1. Make the assignments using the suggested Program Outline/Assignment Sheet, p. 108.
2. Assign the parts for the skit.
3. Schedule practice times for the skit, including a dress rehearsal.
4. Assign the speaker.
5. Assign young women to perform the talent numbers.
6. Talk with your bishopric to ensure their representation at this event.
7. Schedule the church building for the evening of the event, allowing enough time to set up and decorate the afternoon of the event.

SUGGESTIONS FOR DECORATIONS:

1. Set one table up to represent each value. Have the young women display any projects they have made throughout the year that reflect these values. Refer to the "VALUE-able Harvest Talk Presentation" (see pp. 109-110) to create a centerpiece for each table. For example: Set a vase with white daisies on the Faith table, a blue birdhouse on the Divine Nature table and a basket of carrots on the Choice and Accountability table.

2. Set any items that go along with the harvest theme on the refreshment table. For example: Home canned foods, baskets of fresh fruits and vegetables, gourds, flowers, clean gardening gloves, etc.

SUGGESTIONS FOR REFRESHMENTS:

Apple cake with whipped cream and hot apple cider to drink. (Optional: The day of the event, cut the top off and hollow out a pumpkin. Rinse the inside thoroughly. Replace the lid. Set the pumpkin on the refreshment table as a centerpiece. Pour the hot apple cider into the pumpkin just before serving time and use the pumpkin as a punch bowl.)

_____Opening song: "Come, Ye Thankful People," hymnbook, p. 94

_____Opening prayer

_____Welcome: Include the objective of the program.

_____Talent number: Have one or more young women perform a violin or piano solo, sing a song, read a poem she has written, etc.

_____Presentation of "The VALUE-able Harvest" skit

_____Speaker: See the "Celebrate a VALUE-able Harvest" talk presentation, pp. 109-110.

_____Talent number: Have one or more young women perform. Try to make it different from the previous talent number(s).

_____Personal Progress achievement awards: This is the time to acknowledge the progress of each young woman. Give each young woman any Personal Progress certificates or jewelry deserved. Distribute the appropriate "VALUE-able Harvest" garland pieces to each young woman (see p. 133, step #8).

_____Closing song: "Lord, Dismiss Us with Thy Blessing," hymnbook, p. 163

_____Closing prayer and blessing on the refreshments

_____Refreshments: Apple cake with whipped cream and hot apple cider to drink.

More Assignments to Consider

_____Preparation of invitations   _____Refreshments organizer
_____Preparation of programs   _____Decorations organizer
_____Preparation of handouts   _____Setup organizer
_____Skit director/organizer   _____Cleanup organizer

INSTRUCTIONS FOR MAKING THE INVITATIONS, PROGRAMS AND HANDOUTS

INVITATIONS: See p. 120.

PROGRAMS: Make a copy of the program border (p. 122). Write or type your program information inside the border. Copy the program front (p. 121) onto ivory paper with the border on the reverse side of the paper. Fold in half.

HANDOUTS: See p. 133.

The following is an outline for the value talk and goes along with the skit and the handouts. You may want to elaborate on each value as you present your talk.

Faith—Daisy:
A daisy is white like the color for Faith. Its petals are centered around the yellow center. Our faith helps us to know that the gospel is like the daisy petals; it is eternal and it is centered around Christ. If we believe and have faith in Christ, then we will desire to keep his commandments. By keeping his commandments, we will be able to live with him again according to the gospel plan.

Divine Nature—Birdhouse:
The birdhouse is to remind us of birds and the beautiful music they give us. Birds, by nature, are able to sing. Because we are daughters of Heavenly Father, we have divine talents and qualities that are ours just by nature. We may have to listen very closely to the Holy Ghost to know what they are, but as we develop them further we become more like Christ and our Heavenly Father.

Individual Worth—Apple:
There are many different varieties of apples. There are red ones and green ones. Some are tart and are meant for use in baking. Some are sweet and are good for eating. But they all have a purpose. We are like apples in that we are all different in some ways, yet we all have a purpose.

We all have unique talents and qualities and should pray to seek and develop them. We should also share these talents and qualities with others.

Knowledge—Watering Can:
We are like plants. Just as plants need constant watering and feeding or they will die, our minds need constant watering and feeding also. The only thing we can take with us into our next life is our knowledge. This is why it is so important to learn as much as we can now.

Choice and Accountability—Carrot:
A carrot is orange like the color for Choice and Accountability. So, if you "carrot" all about yourself, you will be sure to make wise choices. Remember, you are responsible for the choices you make.

Good Works—Sunflower:
Have you ever seen a sunflower and not smiled? They just seem to be bright and cheery, and they are yellow like the color for Good Works. Heavenly Father wants us to do good works and acts of service for others, and he wants us to do them cheerfully and with a smile. We can be like a sunflower, bright and cheery, as we let our light shine in helping others.

Integrity—Grapes:
As you look at grapes, you will notice they grow in clusters. Each grape is securely attached to the stem. We should be securely attached to a stem also. Our stem should be one of integrity. We should try to cluster all of our thoughts and actions around our stem of integrity. If we do this, we will be honest and upright young women.

110

This skit should be performed in a melodramatic fashion with a lot of overacting and audience participation.

SETTING:
A farm setting (bale of hay, old wooden crates, farm tools, etc.) Miss Farmer can wear country-style clothes, i.e., straw hat, bandanna or scarf, etc., and Miss Banker can wear a black cape. The skit starts with the room lights off and Miss Farmer sleeping on the ground. Miss Banker is off stage.

PROPS:
A white daisy in a glass vase (represents Faith)
A blue bird house (represents Divine Nature)
A red apple (represents Individual Worth)
A green watering can (represents Knowledge)
An orange carrot (represents Choice & Accountability)
A yellow sunflower (represents Good Works)
A cluster of purple grapes (represents Integrity)
Audience participation and song cards, pp. 123-132

PLAYERS:
Narrator - a young woman
Miss Farmer - a young woman
Miss Banker - a young woman
audience participation cardholder / rooster voice - a young woman to hold up the audience participation cards as indicated in the script and to be the voice of the rooster
Song card holders - seven young women (one to hold each card as indicated in the song)
Lighting technician - a young woman or an adult leader to turn the room lights off and on as indicated in the script

NARRATOR:
The sun rises over the farm *(turn lights on)* and the rooster crows *(rooster crows)*, beginning the first day of harvest. Miss Farmer is already up and working very hard on the farm. *(She doesn't get up. The narrator says more loudly...)* Miss Farmer is already up and working very hard on the farm *(she jumps up)* because today is the first day of harvest.

MISS FARMER:
(looking out across the farm) I just know this will be the most VALUE-able harvest ever! *(Hold up YEA! card.)*

NARRATOR:
Hours pass quickly as she works. And at the end of the day she sits among the white daisies and admires them for they always remind her of FAITH. But then—just as she's relaxing, she hears an all-too-familiar, sinister voice. *(Miss Banker enters the stage.)* Yes! It is Miss Banker!

111

MISS BANKER:
Miss Farmer, it's time to collect the mortgage again! *(Hold up BOO! card.)*

MISS FARMER:
Oh my! But I don't have it yet. *(Hold up SIGH... card.)*

NARRATOR:
Miss Farmer explained to Miss Banker that she would be able to pay her when the VALUE-able harvest was over. But Miss Banker wasn't satisfied. She wanted payment now!

MISS BANKER:
Surely you have something you can give me today! *(Hold up BOO! card.)*

MISS FARMER:
I don't know if I have anything to give you today. *(Hold up SIGH... card.)*

NARRATOR:
How about a white daisy in a glass vase?

MISS FARMER:
Oh, I know! I would like you to have this white daisy in a glass vase. It represents FAITH.

NARRATOR:
Miss Banker was satisfied for now, but left with this reply—

MISS BANKER:
I'll be back tomorrow. *(Hold up BOO! card. Miss Banker leaves the stage.)*

NARRATOR:
And so, Miss Farmer goes to bed sad *(she lies down)* because she doesn't know what she can give Miss Banker tomorrow. *(Hold up SIGH... card.)* The sun sets on the farm *(turn lights off)*, ending the first day of harvest.

The sun rises over the farm *(turn lights on)* and the rooster crows *(rooster crows)*, beginning the second day of harvest. It's a beautiful morning, the sun is shining, and the birds are singing. Miss Farmer awakes cheerfully. *(She doesn't get up. The narrator says more loudly...)* Miss Farmer awakes cheerfully *(she gets up)*, for she has forgotten all about Miss Banker.

MISS FARMER:
I'm so happy because I just know this will be the most VALUE-able harvest ever! *(Hold up YEA! card.)*

NARRATOR:

Again, Miss Farmer works on the farm and the hours pass. At the end of the day she sits by the blue birdhouse and listens to the birds sing. Their song reminds her of DIVINE NATURE. She is lost in her thoughts when she is interrupted by Miss Banker. *(Miss Banker enters the stage.)*

MISS BANKER:

Miss Farmer, do you like my new shoes? *(She points to shoes.)* I got them after I foreclosed on my mother! *(She gives a sinister laugh. Hold up BOO! card.)* So, what do you have for me today?

MISS FARMER:

I don't know if I have anything to give you today. *(Hold up SIGH... card.)*

NARRATOR:

How about that blue birdhouse?

MISS FARMER:

Oh, I know! I would like you to have this blue birdhouse. It represents our DIVINE NATURE. *(Hold up YEA! card.)*

NARRATOR:

Miss Banker was satisfied for now, but left with this reply—

MISS BANKER:

I look forward to seeing you again tomorrow! *(She gives a sinister laugh as she leaves the stage. Hold up BOO! card.)*

NARRATOR:

And so, Miss Farmer goes to bed *(Miss Farmer lies down)* sad because she doesn't know what she can give Miss Banker tomorrow. *(Hold up SIGH... card.)* The sun sets *(turn lights off)* on the farm, ending the second day of harvest.

The sun rises *(turn lights on)* over the farm and the rooster crows *(rooster crows)*, beginning the third day of harvest. Wake up, Miss Farmer. *(She doesn't get up. The narrator says more loudly...)* Wake up, Miss Farmer. *(She gets up.)* Today is the day you work in the apple orchard! Miss Farmer is excited, for she has forgotten all about Miss Banker.

MISS FARMER:

I can't wait to go to work in the apple orchard and I just know this will be the most VALUE-able harvest ever! *(Hold up YEA! card.)*

NARRATOR:

What a nice day for Miss Farmer. With each red apple she picks, she is reminded of her INDIVIDUAL WORTH. By the end of the day, she is feeling great. However, her spirits quickly drop. *(Miss Banker enters the stage.)*

MISS BANKER:

Yoo hoo, Miss Farmer! I'm back. Did you miss me? What do you have for me today? *(Hold up BOO! card.)*

MISS FARMER:

I don't know if I have anything to give you today. *(Hold up SIGH... card.)*

NARRATOR:

How about a red apple?

MISS FARMER:

Oh, I know! I want you to have this red apple. It represents our INDIVIDUAL WORTH. *(Hold up YEA! card.)*

NARRATOR:

Miss Banker was satisfied for now, but she left with this reply—

MISS BANKER:

Until tomorrow... too-ta-loo! *(She gives a sinister laugh as she leaves the stage. Hold up BOO! card.)*

NARRATOR:

And so, Miss Farmer goes to bed sad *(she lies down)* because she doesn't know what she can give Miss Banker tomorrow. *(Hold up SIGH... card.)* The sun sets *(turn lights off)* on the farm, ending the third day of harvest.

The sun rises *(turn lights on)* over the farm and the rooster crows *(rooster crows)*, beginning the fourth day of harvest. Miss Farmer wakes up extra early this morning. *(She doesn't get up. Narrator says more loudly...)* Miss Farmer wakes up extra early this morning. *(She still doesn't get up.)* Okay, maybe not extra early but *(loudly...)* she does get up, because today promises to be a scorcher. *(She gets up.)* And a scorcher it is! After a day's work, Miss Farmer takes a break because she is so hot.

MISS FARMER:

Oh my, I'm so hot! I bet my crops are, too! I must water them so that I can have the most VALUE-able harvest ever! *(She uses the green watering can to pretend to water them. Hold up YEA! card.)*

NARRATOR:

And so the crops are restored. Miss Farmer takes a moment to gaze at the green watering can and smiles as she is reminded of KNOWLEDGE. Miss Farmer has forgotten all about Miss Banker, but is soon reminded as she sees her. *(Miss Banker enters the stage.)*

MISS FARMER:

Oh no! I forgot you were coming and I don't know if I have anything to give you today. *(Hold up SIGH... card.)*

MISS BANKER:

That's what my grandmother said last month, right before I evicted her. *(She gives a sinister laugh. Hold up BOO! card.)*

NARRATOR:

How about the green watering can?

MISS FARMER:

Oh, I know! I want you to have this watering can. It represents KNOWLEDGE. *(Hold up YEA! card.)*

NARRATOR:

Miss Banker was satisfied for now but she left with this reply—

MISS BANKER:

Parting is such sweet sorrow—oh well, I'll be back tomorrow! *(She gives a sinister laugh as she leaves the stage. Hold up BOO! card.)*

NARRATOR:

And so, Miss Farmer goes to bed sad *(she lies down)* because she doesn't know what she can give Miss Banker tomorrow. *(Hold up SIGH... card.)* The sun sets *(turn lights off)* on the farm, ending the fourth day of harvest.

The sun rises *(turn lights on)* over the farm and the rooster crows *(rooster crows)*, beginning the fifth day of harvest. Rise and shine, Miss Farmer. *(She jumps right up. Narrator starts to say more loudly...)* Rise and sh— *(Narrator looks and Miss Farmer is up. Narrator is surprised.)* Oh well, where was I? Oh yes, it's time to get to work on your most VALUE-able harvest ever.

MISS FARMER:

I must rise and shine so I can go to work on my most VALUE-able harvest ever. *(Hold up YEA! card.)*

NARRATOR:

Miss Farmer proceeds directly to the carrot patch. Today is carrot day and she will need to pull each and every one. Hours pass and afternoon is quickly here. Miss Farmer sits and eats a carrot. As she is biting into an extra crunchy orange carrot, she is reminded of CHOICE and ACCOUNTABILITY. Miss Farmer is very content, for she has forgotten all about Miss Banker. But Miss Banker has not forgotten about her. As a matter of fact—here she comes now! *(Miss Banker enters the stage.)*

MISS FARMER:
Miss Banker, you're here. Oh no! I don't know if I have anything to give you today. *(Hold up SIGH... card.)*

NARRATOR:
How about a crunchy orange carrot?

MISS FARMER:
Oh, I know! I want you to have a crunchy orange carrot. It represents CHOICE and ACCOUNTABILITY. *(Hold up YEA! card.)*

NARRATOR:
Miss Banker was satisfied for now, but left with this reply—

MISS BANKER:
Tomorrow—same time, same place. *(She gives a sinister laugh as she leaves the stage. Hold up BOO! card.)*

NARRATOR:
And so, Miss Farmer goes to bed *(she lies down)* sad because she doesn't know what she can give Miss Banker tomorrow. *(Hold up SIGH... card.)* The sun sets *(turn lights off)* on the farm, ending the fifth day of harvest.

NARRATOR:
The sun rises *(turn lights on)* over the farm and the rooster crows *(rooster crows)*, beginning the sixth day of harvest. Miss Farmer wakes up cheerfully and early this morning *(She sits partway up and says...)*

MISS FARMER:
Is it time for school already, Mom?

NARRATOR:
Okay, flashback! Remember, the farm and the most VALUE-able harvest ever! Sound familiar?

MISS FARMER:
Oh yes, I remember. I will wake up cheerfully and work on the farm because I know this will be the most VALUE-able harvest ever! *(Hold up YEA! card.)*

NARRATOR:
Hours have passed. Miss Farmer has worked very hard. She is hot and tired. She spots the tall yellow sunflowers swaying in the breeze and sits under them. Cool now from their shade, she is reminded of GOOD WORKS. Once again, she has forgotten all about Miss Banker. *(Miss Banker enters the stage.)*

MISS BANKER:

Miss Farmer, it's me again! What do you have for me today? *(Hold up the BOO! card.)*

MISS FARMER:

I don't know what I have to give you today. *(Hold up SIGH... card.)*

NARRATOR:

How about a swaying yellow sunflower?

MISS FARMER:

Oh, I know! I want you to have this swaying yellow sunflower. It represents GOOD WORKS. *(Hold up YEA! card.)*

MISS BANKER:

Sunflowers, carrots, watering cans—these are all such odd gifts. What am I supposed to do with them?

MISS FARMER:

I'm only looking out for your best interest. That's why I want you to have all these gifts. *(Hold up YEA! card.)*

MISS BANKER:

Interest..., yes interest! I knew there was something I forgot to add to your bill! I'll be back tomorrow with the mortgage bill. *(She gives a sinister laugh as she leaves the stage. Hold up BOO! card.)*

NARRATOR:

And so, Miss Farmer goes to bed sad *(she lies down)* because she doesn't know what she can give Miss Banker tomorrow. *(Hold up SIGH... card.)* The sun sets *(turn lights off)* on the farm, ending the sixth day of harvest.

The sun rises *(turn lights on)* over the farm and the rooster crows *(rooster crows)*, beginning the seventh day of harvest. Miss Farmer rises early. *(She doesn't get up.)* Oh well, she's really tired. We'll let her sleep in for a while longer. *(Miss Banker enters the stage and begins to pace back and forth.)* Meanwhile, Miss Banker has been up all night pacing the floor wondering why these gifts are so important that Miss Farmer would want her to have them.

MISS BANKER:

I wish I could understand why these gifts are so important. *(Hold up SIGH... card.)*

NARRATOR:

She paces and paces and paces until finally she understands. *(Miss Farmer gets up and pretends to pick grapes.)*

MISS BANKER:
Finally I understand! *(Hold up YEA! card.)* I must hurry and go tell Miss Farmer.

NARRATOR:
Miss Farmer has since gotten up and is picking grapes. She is always reminded of INTEGRITY when she picks purple grapes. Miss Farmer notices Miss Banker, and she is ready with a gift today.

MISS FARMER:
Miss Banker, you're early today. Luckily, I do know what I can give you today. I would like you to have this bunch of purple grapes. They represent INTEGRITY! *(Hold up YEA! card.)*

MISS BANKER:
Thank you for pointing out all these gifts to me. I understand now! *(Hold up YEA! card.)*

NARRATOR:
Miss Banker now realizes that each of these gifts—FAITH, DIVINE NATURE, INDIVIDUAL WORTH, KNOWLEDGE, CHOICE and ACCOUNTABILITY, GOOD WORKS and INTEGRITY—have always been hers. She just needed to recognize them and to work hard to develop them.

MISS FARMER:
The harvest is over and now I can pay the mortgage. *(Hold up YEA! card.)*

MISS BANKER:
You were right—

BOTH TOGETHER:
This was the most VALUE-able harvest ever! *(Hold up YEA! card.)*

NARRATOR:
(talking to the audience) Please join with us and sing the "Seven Days of Harvest" sung to the tune of the "Twelve days of Christmas."

SONG: "Seven Days of Harvest," see p. 119
(The seven young women who are holding the song cards line up and face the audience.)

NARRATOR:
And so, both Miss Farmer and Miss Banker go to sleep happy that night. *(They both lie down.)* The sun sets *(turn lights off)* on the farm, ending the seventh day of the most VALUE-able harvest ever! *(Hold up Yea! card.)*

SONG: *"The Seven Days of Harvest"*

On the first day of harvest, Miss Farmer gave to me...
A daisy in a glass vase *(hold up daisy card)*.

On the second day of harvest, Miss Farmer gave to me...
Two birdhouses *(hold up birdhouse card)*
And a daisy in a glass vase *(hold up daisy card)*.

On the third day of harvest, Miss Farmer gave to me...
Three red apples *(hold up apple card)*
Two birdhouses *(hold up birdhouse card)*
And a daisy in a glass vase *(hold up daisy card)*.

On the fourth day of harvest, Miss Farmer gave to me...
Four water cans *(hold up watering can card)*
Three red apples *(hold up apple card)*
Two birdhouses *(hold up birdhouse card)*
and a daisy in a glass vase *(hold up daisy card)*.

On the fifth day of harvest, Miss Farmer gave to me...
Five crunchy carrots *(hold up carrot card)*
Four water cans *(hold up watering can card)*
Three red apples *(hold up apple card)*
Two birdhouses *(hold up birdhouse card)*
And a daisy in a glass vase *(hold up daisy card)*.

On the sixth day of harvest, Miss Farmer gave to me...
Six sunflowers swaying *(hold up sunflower card)*
Five crunchy carrots *(hold up carrot card)*
Four water cans *(hold up watering can card)*
Three red apples *(hold up apple card)*
Two birdhouses *(hold up birdhouse card)*
And a daisy in a glass vase *(hold up daisy card)*.

On the seventh day of harvest, Miss Farmer gave to me...
Seven grapes in bunches *(hold up grapes card)*
Six sunflowers swaying *(hold up sunflower card)*
Five crunchy carrots *(hold up carrot card)*
Four water cans *(hold up watering can card)*
Three red apples *(hold up apple card)*
Two birdhouses *(hold up birdhouse card)*
And a daisy in a glass vase *(hold up daisy card)*.

Church
dress please.

Come fill your
spiritual basket.

Refreshments
will be served.

Celebrate a
VALUE-able Harvest

You and your parents
are invited
to come and

EVENING OF EXCELLENCE

cut

HOW TO MAKE THE INVITATIONS:

Make a copy of this page. Write or type your information on the apple pull tab below. Copy the invitation onto tan colored paper. Cut the basket section out along the outside border. Cut a slit in the basket where indicated. Fold the basket section in half. Cut out the apple pull tab below. Insert the apple pull tab through the slit in the basket so that the apple shows and the information is hidden between the two layers of the invitation. Carefully glue the bottom and sides of the basket section together. Slide the apple up and down to read the information. (Optional: Use colored pencils to color all the apples red, the stems brown and the leaves green. Glue a raffia bow at the top of the basket handle on the front side of the invitation.)

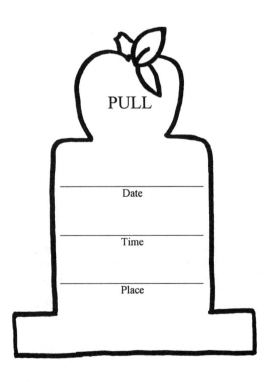

PULL

Date

Time

Place

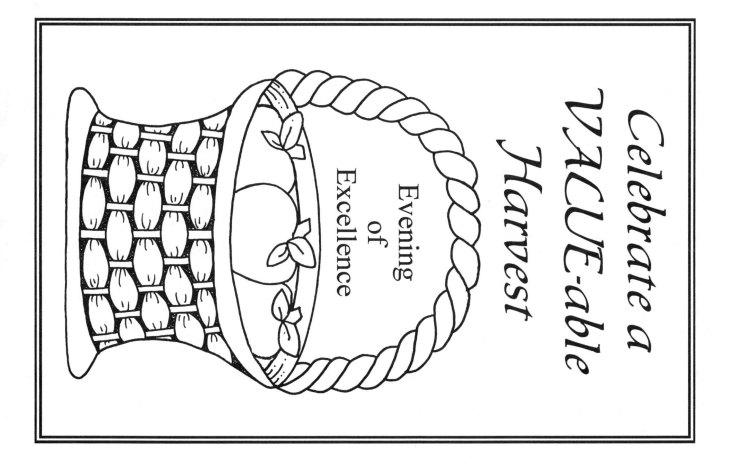

Celebrate a
VACUE-able
Harvest

Evening
of
Excellence

VEA¡
APPCAUSE

SIGH...

A DAISY
IN A
GLASS
VASE

3

RED
APPLES

5 CRUNCHY CARROTS

SUNFLOWERS SWAYING

9

7

GRAPES IN BUNCHES

The young women would have fun making the objects for their own garland handout at mid-week activities. (Be sure to schedule 3-4 activities throughout the year, prior to the Evening of Excellence event.) As they finish each object, they will give them back to you. You will keep them and hand them out at the Evening of Excellence event.

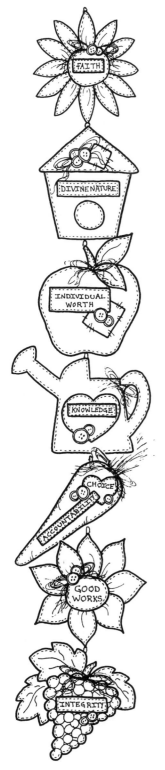

For each object: (see patterns, pp. 134-140)

1. Cut a 7" x 7" piece of thin brown corrugated cardboard. (Hint: Pizza delivery boxes work well. You may be able to purchase some from a local pizza establishment for very little cost, or even have them donated.)

2. Refer to pattern to cut the fabric and paper pieces.

3. Use a small paintbrush to apply white craft glue to the back of the "body" piece; center it on the cardboard piece. Using the same method, glue each pattern piece on the "body" as indicated in the pattern; let dry.

4. Use pinking shears to cut the cardboard closely around the object.

5. Use a medium-tip black permanent pen to outline and detail the object as indicated on the pattern. Use a fine-tip black permanent pen to add the value lettering and details to the object as indicated on the pattern.

6. Tie a small bow from natural raffia. Use hot glue to glue the bow where indicated on the pattern. Use hot glue to glue buttons to the object as indicated on the pattern.

7. Bend a 2" wire length into a "U" shape. Bend a 2" wire length into a "hook" shape. Glue the "U" upside down to the back of the object at the top to form a hanger and the "hook" at the bottom so the object will hang together with the others in a garland as shown to the left. (You will not need a "hook" on the grapes.)

8. At the Evening of Excellence event: Give each young woman the objects that she has earned. For example: If she has finished both value experiences in faith, give her a daisy. If she has finished both value experiences in all seven of the values, give her one of each object. If she does not receive all the objects that night, she will be able to add to her garland later as she completes her value experiences.

"pattern"
refer to this to assemble
the daisy

"value"
cut 1 from
brown craft paper

"center"
cut 1 from
yellow floral fabric

"body"
cut 1 from
white fabric

FAITH

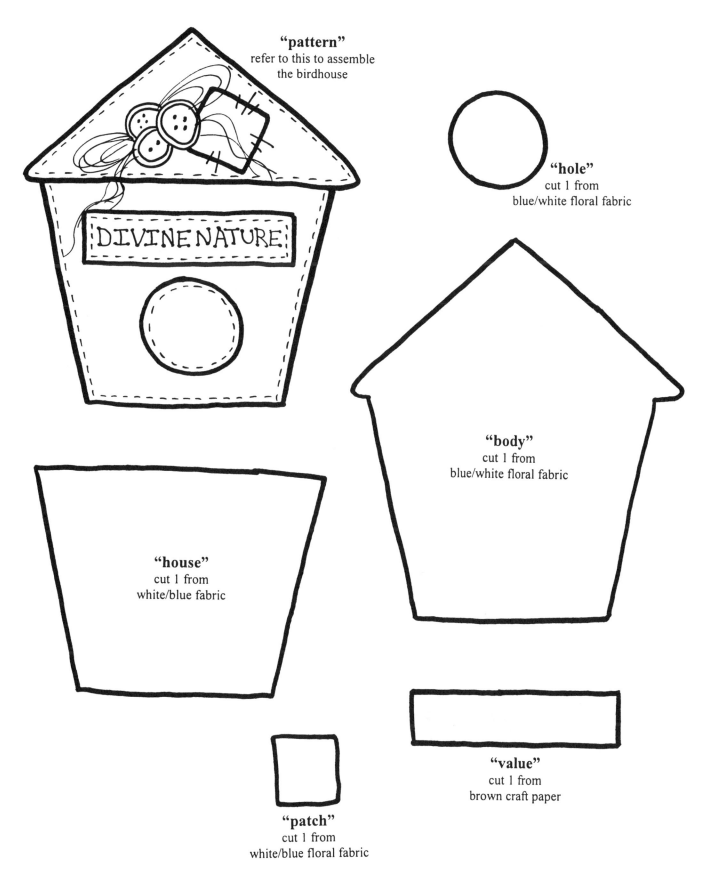

"pattern"
refer to this to assemble
the birdhouse

DIVINE NATURE

"hole"
cut 1 from
blue/white floral fabric

"body"
cut 1 from
blue/white floral fabric

"house"
cut 1 from
white/blue fabric

"value"
cut 1 from
brown craft paper

"patch"
cut 1 from
white/blue floral fabric

"pattern"
refer to this to assemble
the apple

"patch"
cut 1 from
white/red checked fabric

INDIVIDUAL
WORTH

"body"
cut 1 from
red/white floral fabric

"value"
cut 1 from
brown craft paper

"leaves"
cut 1 from
green floral fabric

"stem"
cut 1 from
beige floral fabric

"pattern"
refer to this to assemble
the watering can

KNOWLEDGE

"value"
cut 1 from
brown craft paper

"heart"
cut 1 from
beige floral fabric

"body"
cut 1 from
green floral fabric

*Use hot glue to glue several thin green raffia strands extending out from the carrot end.

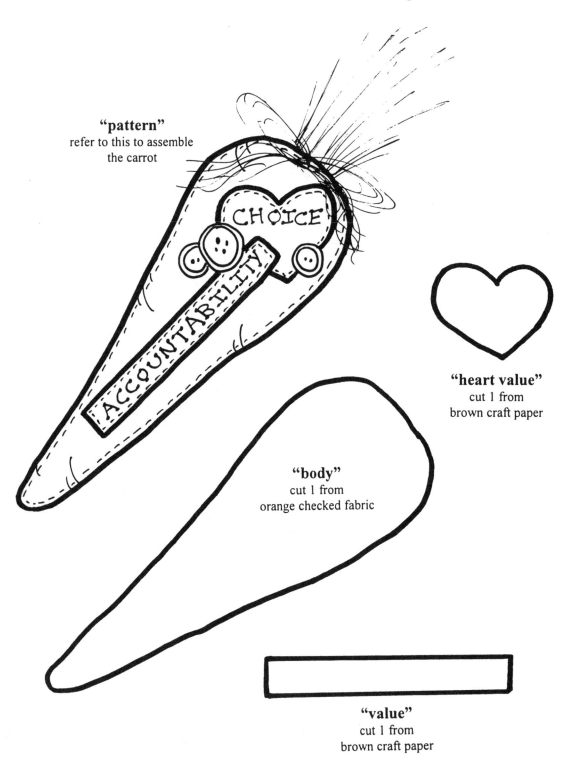

"pattern"
refer to this to assemble
the carrot

"heart value"
cut 1 from
brown craft paper

"body"
cut 1 from
orange checked fabric

"value"
cut 1 from
brown craft paper

"pattern"
refer to this to assemble
the sunflower

GOOD
WORKS

"center value"
cut 1 from
brown craft paper

"body"
cut 1 from
yellow floral fabric

"pattern"
refer to this to assemble
the grapes

INTEGRITY

"grapes"
cut 1 from
purple floral fabric

"body"
cut 1 from
green floral fabric

"stem"
cut 1 from
beige floral fabric

"value"
cut 1 from
brown craft paper